I0759495

THE 10TH MOUNTAIN DIVISION IN WORLD WAR II

CASEMATE | ILLUSTRATED | SPECIAL

CASEMATE | ILLUSTRATED | SPECIAL

THE 10TH MOUNTAIN DIVISION IN WORLD WAR II

EQUIPMENT AND VEHICLES

CHARLES C. ROBERTS, Jr.

CIS0024

Published in 2025 by
CASEMATE PUBLISHERS
1950 Lawrence Road, Havertown, PA 19083, USA
and
47 Church Street, Barnsley, S70 2AS, UK

Print Edition: ISBN 978-1-63624-605-5
Digital Edition: ISBN 978-1-63624-606-2

Design by Battlefield Design
Printed and bound in the Czech Republic by FINIDR s.r.o.

CASEMATE PUBLISHERS (US)
Telephone (610) 853-9131
Fax (610) 853-9146
Email: casemate@casematepublishers.com
www.casematepublishers.com

CASEMATE PUBLISHERS (UK)
Telephone (0)1226 734350
Email: casemate@casemateuk.com
www.casemateuk.com

Acknowledgements: I would like to thank the following people for their work on the book: John Adams-Graf, reviewer and photo contributor; Jeremiah Harris, reviewer and photo contributor; Mike Krizsanitz, reviewer; Dave Little, reviewer and photo contributor; Lydia Roberts, draft editor; Sepp Scanlin, reviewer and photo contributor; Flint Whitlock, reviewer and photo contributor; Jeff Wzolek, reviewer and photo contributor.

Unless stated otherwise, images are from the author's collection.

Front cover images: M29C Weasel in winter; 77 mm pack howitzer; "Hall Burton, mountain trooper, carrying a full pack and rifle, exhibits his skill on skis. Camp Hale, Colo" (Signal Corps); M3 37 mm gun on skis. (John Adams-Graf)
Back cover images: ski trooper reenactor skiing with original 10th Mountain Division equipment; the ice axe, an essential tool for mountaineering; troops of G Company, 2nd Battalion, 10th Mountain Division march down the street in newly liberated Verona, Italy, on April 26, 1945 (John Adams-Graf); restored M7 Snow Tractor, serial number 283.
Title page image: Landing supplies on Kiska. The Weasel at the right is towing an Athey 6-ton Tracked Trailer, probably secured from another unit. (John Adams-Graf)
Contents page images: foreground, M28 Weasel at Camp Hale. The M28, like other Weasels, was a prime mover for towing sleds and skiers (John Adams-Graf); background, troops of G Company, 2nd Battalion, 10th Mountain Division march down the street in newly liberated Verona, Italy, on April 26, 1945. Note the 1943 jungle packs used by the 10th instead of the mountain rucksacks. (John Adams-Graf)

Contents

10th training at Red Cliff, Colorado. (John Adams-Graf)

Evacuating wounded at Riva Ridge by cable lift. (National Archives)

Timeline of Events

November 5, 1940: U.S. War Department forms ski patrol units.

March 1941: Lt. John Woodward leads 41st Division ski patrol maneuvers in the Olympic Mountains.

November 15, 1941: Activation of the 87th Mountain Infantry Regiment.

December 7, 1941: The Japanese attack Pearl Harbor; enlistments flood the 87th.

May–June 1942: 2nd Battalion 87th and 3rd Battalion 87th activated.

June 1942: Japanese forces occupy Aleutian Islands, Alaska.

July–August 1942: A detachment from the 87th tests snow vehicles in the Columbia Ice Fields.

September 3, 1942: The Mountain Training Center (MTC) is activated at Camp Carson, Colorado.

November 16, 1942: The MTC moves to Camp Hale with one regiment, the 87th.

Jeep and soldier at Camp Hale. (John Adams-Graf)

June 13, 1943: The 87th Regiment undergoes amphibious training for the Aleutian Islands mission.

July 15, 1943: The 10th Light Division (Alpine) is activated at Camp Hale.

August 15–16, 1943: The 87th lands on Kiska, Alaska, and secures the island along with other units.

February 23, 1944: The 87th rejoins the 10th Light Division at Camp Hale.

March–May 1944: The 10th Light Division undergoes D-Series maneuvers to test readiness.

June 20–24, 1944: The 10th Light Division leaves for Camp Swift, Texas, for flatland training.

November 6, 1944: The 10th Light Division is reorganized as the 10th Mountain Division.

November 23, 1944: Brig. Gen. George P. Hays takes command of the division.

January 8–11, 1945: Hays arrives in Italy and meets with Gen. Truscott to plan attacks.

January 20, 1945: The whole division is now in Italy preparing for action.

February 18–19, 1945: Units of the 86th assault and secure Riva Ridge.

February 19–24, 1945: The entire division assaults and secures Monte Belvedere and Monte Gorgolesco.

April 16, 1945: The 87th captures Tole moving toward the Po Valley.

April 20, 1945: The 10th breaks out of the Apennines into the Po Valley.

April 23, 1945: The 87th and 85th cross the Po River under fire.

April 27, 1945: The division leapfrogs along the shores of Lake Garda, chasing the Germans.

April 30, 1945: The division takes Torbole and heads toward Riva; DUKW sinks, loss of 25 men.

May 2, 1945: German army in Italy surrenders.

May 7, 1945: Germany surrenders.

Military transport ship at Kiska.

Kiska camp.

751st Tank Battalion on Monte Belvedere. (National Archives)

Introduction

The 10th Division was initially organized in July 1918 during World War I as a division in the Regular Army and the National Army but was never deployed overseas. During the Soviet Union's invasion of Finland in November 1939, Finnish soldiers on skis destroyed two Red Army armored divisions. The conflict attracted global attention as the outnumbered and outgunned Finnish soldiers were able to use the difficult local terrain to their advantage, severely hampering the Soviet attacks.

Upon seeing the effectiveness of these troops, Charles Minot "Minnie" Dole, the president and founder of the National Ski Patrol, began to lobby the War Department for the need for a similar unit of troops trained for fighting in winter and mountain warfare in the United States Army. In September 1940, Dole presented his case to Army Chief of Staff General George C. Marshall. Marshall agreed to create a "mountain" unit for fighting in harsh terrain. On October 20, 1941, the War Department authorized Dole's group, the National Volunteer Winter Defense Committee, as the official recruiter for a special mountain-trained unit. In 1940, Roger Langley, Alexander Bright, Robert Livermore, and Minnie Dole, all accomplished skiers, discussed the formation of a mountain troop division in the U.S. Army.

The concern was that the United States was vulnerable to attack by ski troops from the north since it appeared that the United States would be drawn into a global conflict that had begun in Europe. Dick Durance was teaching skiing to members of parachute battalions—the only mountain-related training performed in the U.S. Army. Roger Langley, president of the National Ski Association, offered the services of the National Ski Patrol and the National Ski Association to the War Department to develop mountain fighting capability. Major General Simon Buckner, commander of the Alaska Defense Command, needed cold-weather clothing and equipment to operate in the cold climate of Alaska. II Corps commander General Phillipson felt that German units could attack from the north and that U.S. units should be trained in cold-weather and mountain warfare. The U.S. Army finally relented by making plans to station five divisions in the north that were trained to operate in "winter conditions." A small-unit ski patrol was to be attached to each division under the tutelage of the National Ski Patrol. In 1941, these five experimental ski patrols trained during the winter, demonstrating the feasibility of forming a whole mountain division.

In the winter of 1941/42, the 87th Mountain Infantry was formed under the command of Colonel Onslow S. Rolfe, with the National Ski Patrol and American Alpine Club helping recruit members. The unit was initially stationed at Fort Lewis, Washington, but later moved to Mt. Rainer and Camp Hale at Pando, Colorado. Early in the recruitment process, skiing ability was required. It was thought that it was easier to train skiers how to be soldiers than to train soldiers how to ski.

Constituted on July 10, 1943, the 10th Light Division (Alpine) was activated five days later at Camp Hale, centered on regimental commands: the 85th, 86th, and 87th Infantry Regiments. Also assigned to the Division were the 604th, 605th, and 616th Field Artillery Battalions, the 110th Signal Company, the 710th Ordnance Company, the 10th Quartermaster Company, the 10th Reconnaissance Troop, the 126th Engineer Battalion, the 10th Medical Battalion, and the 10th Counter-Intelligence Detachment. In August 1943, the 87th Regiment participated in Operation *Cottage*, the invasion of the island of Kiska in the Aleutians. On November 6, 1944, the 10th Light Division was redesignated the 10th Mountain Division.

By 1943, the Quartermaster Supply Catalog contained equipment germane to the mountain troops, such as skis, ski boots, ski poles, mountain tents, and other equipment. Weapons the 10th Mountain Division used were typical of those provided to light infantry divisions, such as the M1 rifle, M1903 rifle, M1911 pistol, and others.

The Studebaker Corporation developed the M29 Carrier (Weasel) in 1942 as a vehicle for special forces to attack facilities in Norway. The 10th Mountain Division adopted the vehicle as the primary carrier for transport over mountainous terrain with snowy conditions. The Weasel was used in the Kiska operation and in Italy. The ubiquitous MB/GPW Jeep was supplied to the 10th Mountain Division and used in Italy. Several other vehicles were tested at Camp Hale, such as the T16 snow tractor, the M7 snow tractor, and several motorized toboggans, which the 10th Mountain Division did not use in combat.

Several artillery battalions with pack howitzers were attached to the 10th Mountain Division. The 10th Mountain Division also utilized vehicles from support units such as the Higgins Boat from the U.S. Navy during the Kiska operation, the DUKW "Duck" for crossing rivers and lakes in Italy, the 2½-ton cargo truck, and the WC51 ¾-ton truck. This book describes the unique equipment used by the 10th Mountain Division and equipment that was evaluated but not used.

Camp Hale, October 1942. (John Adams-Graf)

The 10th Mountain Division in World War II

In January 1940, Assistant Secretary of War Louis Johnson asked General George C. Marshall about providing winter clothing and equipment to infantry units to match the effectiveness of the Finnish troops in their battles in northern Russia. The American Alpine Club recommended mountain warfare training be part of the preparation for war in the U.S. Army. In September of 1940, Charles Minot Dole, chairman of the National Ski Patrol Committee of the National Ski Association, met with General Marshall and insisted that infantry units use proper mountaineering and skiing equipment, and any decisions on the nature of the equipment should be made after consulting with those experienced with mountain operations. In November of 1940, the War Department formed ski patrol units in the 1st, 3rd, 5th, 6th, 41st, and 44th Divisions. The 1st Division started training in New York at Plattsburg Barracks and Lake Placid. Members of the National Ski Association visited winter training sites for the divisions and advised on winter operations. Lieutenant John Woodward, famed skier and mountaineer, led a patrol around Mt. Rainer and later, in March 1941, led a two-week winter maneuver into the Olympic Mountains in Washington. In April 1941, Colonels Walker and Hurdis were charged with finding a location capable of housing 15,000 men suitable for year-round training. Minot Dole and the National Ski Patrol established entry requirements for men joining a winter warfare division, which included three letters of recommendation attesting to a recruit's level of competence in mountaineering or skiing. Over 7,000 men were recruited.

Training of 10th Mountain Division ski troops at Camp Hale. (John Adams-Graf)

Amphibious Task Force 9 landing on a Kiska beach. (U.S. Army)

The attack on Pearl Harbor by the Japanese Navy resulted in the activation of additional battalions of the 87th Mountain Infantry Regiment at Fort Lewis, Washington, because of a significant number of recruits willing to serve. In March 1942, the War Department was reorganized, placing Lieutenant General McNair in charge of training all ground troops in the U.S. Army. McNair supported the activation of the 87th, which led to the construction of Camp Hale in Pando, Colorado, named after General Irving Hale, former commander of the Colorado National Guard. The 1st Battalion of the 87th Infantry Regiment was activated at Camp Hale in November 1942, with the second and third battalions not fully constituted because of budgetary restraints.

In June 1942, Japanese forces invaded and occupied the Aleutian Islands of Kiska and Attu in Alaska. This operation by the Japanese was to create a diversion for the U.S. Navy while the Japanese were approaching Midway Island in the Pacific. The Japanese wanted to motivate the U.S. Navy to sail north to retake the Aleutian Islands, leaving Midway Island vulnerable. This would clear the way for the Japanese to occupy Midway and make it a base to deter further attacks on Japan, such as the Doolittle Raid, which had been a huge embarrassment to the Japanese. The Japanese naval code had been broken by the U.S. Navy, indicating that the real target was Midway Island. American forces did not fall for the diversion, resulting in a significant victory at the Battle of Midway.

10th Mountain patrol scouting the area around Riva Ridge. (National Archives)

In December 1942, the 99th Infantry Battalion, composed of first- and second-generation Norwegians, arrived at Camp Hale to be trained in mountain warfare alongside the 10th. In May 1943, the 7th Infantry Division landed at Attu to take back the Aleutian Islands, meeting with significant resistance for 18 days, with over 500 American soldiers killed. In June 1943, the 87th Regiment moved to Fort Ord, California, for amphibious training in anticipation of an attack on the island of Kiska in the Aleutians.

The 10th Light Division (Alpine, Pack), activated in July 1943, included the 85th, 86th, and 87th Infantry Regiments. The training of the ski troops included skiing, snowshoeing, climbing, rappelling, cold-climate survival, high-altitude endurance exercises, and weapons handling in a mountain environment. Early on, soldiers assigned to the division were good skiers, but by 1944, many of the replacement soldiers could not ski. The 87th Mountain Infantry Regiment performed the first combat operation on the island of Kiska before the 10th Light Division was activated. The retaking of the Kiska Island was assigned to Amphibious Task Force 9 and included the 87th Mountain Infantry, one of a few fully trained units available for the task. The 87th landed at Kiska in August 1943, but the Japanese had evacuated the island under the cover of fog, leaving much of their equipment behind. Unfortunately, there were over 300 Allied casualties because of Japanese booby-traps and friendly-fire confusion because of the fog and harsh weather.

After the Kiska operation, the 87th Infantry became the core of the 10th Light Division (Alpine, Pack), eventually becoming the 10th Mountain Division in 1944. From March 24–May 6, 1944, practice maneuvers to test the ability and endurance of 10th Mountain soldiers, called the D-Series maneuvers, took place in the

Map of the route of the 10th in Italy. The route's starting point was January 18, 1945, and the endpoint May 2, 1945 (after Torbole was taken) when the German army in Italy surrendered.

mountain terrain around Camp Hale. One result of the D-Series was the recommendation to Chief of Staff George Marshall that the 10th Light Division become a regular infantry division. During World War II, the 10th Mountain Division became the only U.S. military unit trained for mountain warfare. The division traveled to Camp Swift, Texas, June 20–24, 1944, for additional combat training before an overseas assignment. On November 23, 1944, Brigadier General George P. Hays (soon to be promoted to major general) took command of the 10th at Camp Swift. He had been awarded the Medal of Honor in World War I and had just returned from overseas after commanding the 2nd Infantry Division artillery on Omaha Beach during the Normandy landings in June 1944.

On November 6, 1944, the 10th Light Division was renamed the 10th Mountain Division. The 86th Regiment of the 10th Mountain Division embarked for Italy on December 11, 1944, and was assigned to the Fifth Army under General Mark Clark. The 85th and 87th Regiments embarked for Italy on January 4, 1945. The Germans were dug in on defensive mountain positions in Northern Italy. This was hampering the northern movement of the Fifth Army, and the 10th was needed to root out the Germans. The first significant battle involving the 10th Mountain Division was the assault on Riva Ridge, February 18–19, 1945. Riva Ridge is a series of mountains starting from south to north as LoPiagge, Cingio del Buro, Monte Mancinello, Monte Riva, Monte Serrasiccia, Monte Cappel Buso, and Pizzo di Campiano. It is approximately three and a half mi. long, and was a vantage point for German observers to adjust artillery fire on Allied forces below; it had to be neutralized before any other movement north. Hays met with General L. K. Truscott, Jr., the new commander of the Fifth Army, to discuss the mission of the 10th. Truscott presented his plan to have the 10th capture Monte Belvedere and then proceed to capture all the high ground to a position east of Tole. On the night of February 18/19, the 86th Infantry Regiment of the 10th Mountain Division quietly started climbing the slope of Riva Ridge. The soldiers used all the mountaineering skills they had developed at Camp Hale to climb the cliffs using pitons, ropes, pickaxes, implementing their knowledge of Alpine warfare. The Germans thought the difficult climb up the slope could not be performed, especially at night, and were taken by surprise by the 10th troops such that intense hand-to-hand combat ensued. By the morning of February 19, Riva Ridge was in the hands of the 10th, and the German artillery observers were eliminated. The battle demonstrated the mountaineering skills of the 10th and instilled confidence in the troops.

There was no time to rest because the next assignment was to capture Monte Belvedere. The German 4th Parachute and 232nd Infantry Divisions

Night firing during the assault on Monte Belvedere. (National Archives)

controlled the high ground, including Monte Belvedere, Monte Gorgolesco, and Monte della Torraccia. Monte Belvedere overlooked the highway to Bologna, an important route north. In the past, Monte Belvedere had been defended by artillery fire from Riva Ridge, resulting in unsuccessful attempts to capture it. Now that Riva Ridge was secured, there was less exposure from German artillery fire on the 10th Mountain Division troops moving up. The 85th, 86th, and 87th Mountain Infantry Regiments of the 10th attacked Monte Belvedere and Monte Gorgolesco during the night of February 19/20. On February 20, the 85th carried an attack along the ridge to Monte della Torraccia, and despite significant resistance, they secured the objective on February 24. In March, the 87th captured the crossroads at Castel d'Aiano, and the 85th captured Monte della Spe. By cutting the main line of German communications, the Fifth Army secured control of Route 64, a main route to the Po Valley. This set up the division for the spring offensive.

On April 14, 1945, the spring offensive began with the 10th attacking German positions on the hills north of Monte della Spe. The resistance was significant, and it was the bloodiest day experienced by the 10th in World War II. The spring offensive cost 286 KIA, 1,047 WIA, and 3 POW. By April 17, the German defensive line was broken when the 87th captured Tole, leading to operations on gentler terrain toward the Po Valley.

On April 20, the 10th broke out from the Apennines into the Po Valley. General Hays ordered Brigadier General Robinson E. Duff (second in command) to form Task Force Duff and drive toward the Po River. The Germans were now in a rapid retreat, chased by Task Force Duff. On April 22, Duff was seriously wounded, and Colonel Darby took over, heading up Task Force Darby. On April 23, Task Force Darby reached the Po River and set up a defensive position at a crossing. At noon that day, the 87th crossed the Po under fire, with the help of the 126th Engineers using their assault boats. On April 25, Task Force Darby consisted of the 86th, the 13th Tank Battalion, Company B of the 751st Tank Battalion, Company B of the 701st Tank Destroyer Battalion, the 112th Armored Field Artillery Battalion, and elements of the 126th Engineers, along with the 85th in Villafranca later in the day. On April 26, the task force captured Lazise on the shore of Lake Garda. On April 27, General Hays led the division along the shores of Lake Garda toward Torbole. The Germans had blocked the highway tunnels along the edge of the lake using explosives, necessitating using DUKWs on Lake Garda to transport troops and equipment to the next objective. On April 30, the task force took Torbole and made for the town of Riva. The 10th secured Mussolini's country home, Villa Feltrinelli, in Gargnano. On the evening of April 30, several DUKWs of 10th troops set sail across Lake Garda to the next objective. A storm brewed up,

M4 medium tank firing on positions near Monte Belvedere. (National Archives)

M4 medium tanks that were destroyed in the first attempts to take Monte Belvedere in the fall of 1944. (U.S. Army)

and one DUKW sank with the loss of 25 men, but one survived, Corporal Thomas H. Hough. Finally, on May 2, 1945, all German forces in Italy surrendered. On May 7, Germany surrendered unconditionally, ending World War II in Europe.

On July 14, 1945, the 10th Mountain Division was ordered back to the States to prepare for the invasion of Japan. The plan was for the 10th to attack Kyushu on November 2, 1945. On August 15, 1945, Japan surrendered after the two atomic bomb attacks. On November 30, 1945, the 10th Mountain Division was deactivated.

A total of 22,080 men fought with the 10th in World War II. Exactly 1,000 were KIA between Kiska and Italy. A further 3,683 were wounded (7 on Kiska and 3,676 in Italy); 181 were wounded multiple times: 177 twice, 3 three times, 1 four times, for a total of 3,860 Purple Hearts in combat in Italy. The total number of casualties experienced by the 10th Mountain Division (KIA + WIA) was 4,683, of which 4,653 occurred in Italy.

Moving casualties, March 1945. (National Archives)

Clothing of the 10th Mountain Division

The 10th Mountain Division used a variety of uniforms because of its mission of both infantry and mountain operations. This chapter deals with the divisional uniforms of that era used by the 10th Mountain Division along with the specialized uniforms for mountain operations, including the M1 helmet, Jeep cap, winter cap, coveralls, ski cap, leggings, ski trousers, parkas, mountain jacket, goggles, socks, gloves, service shoes, gaiters, HBTs (herringbone twill), and summer and winter service uniforms.

M1 Helmet

Before the beginning of World War II, the U.S. Army had the M1917 helmets left over from World War I. They were designed to protect soldiers in trenches from shrapnel and debris from above but lacked protection laterally. Early redesigns resulted in a helmet resembling the German *Stahlhelm*, which was considered unacceptable. The infantry board researched several designs and settled on a dome-shaped helmet that generally followed the contour of the head. The helmet extended downward to protect the forehead without hampering vision; the sides were extended downward as far as possible without interfering with weapons firing. The back of the helmet was extended downward to the point where if in the prone position, the helmet would not push forward over the eyes (which did happen to some soldiers).

There were two major manufacturers of the M1 steel helmet body (pot) during World War II: McCord Radiator Manufacturing and Schlueter Manufacturing. Production started in April 1941. Over 22 million M1 helmets were produced during the war. The edging seam was at the front of the helmet but moved to the back of the helmet near the end of the war to prevent facial injury if the seam parted. Many times, soldiers used the steel pot as a washbasin and for cooking.

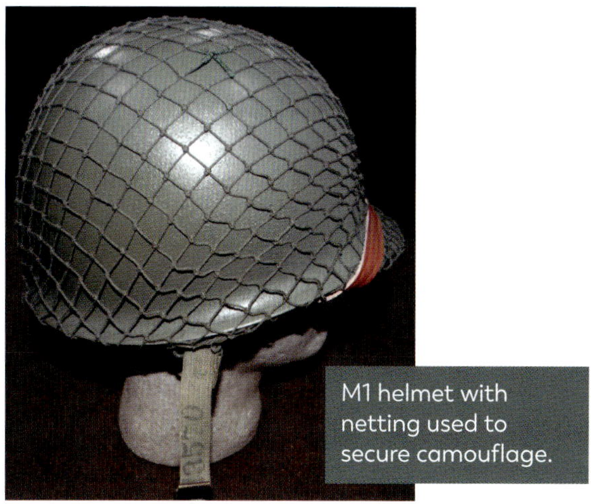

M1 helmet with netting used to secure camouflage.

Schlueter Manufacturing front-edging spot weld at the seam.

McCord Manufacturing front-edging seam spot weld.

M1 helmet liner removed from the steel pot. The liner has a headband and a leather strap to help secure it to the metal pot. It is made from a phenolic material. Toilet paper, if available, was sandwiched between the liner and helmet. A World War II helmet liner had a frontal eyelet hole for insignia. Helmet liners were produced by Westinghouse, Firestone, CAPAC Manufacturing, Inland, Mine Safety Appliances, Seaman Paper Company, and International Molded Plastics.

Helmet liner with headband that could be adjusted to the soldier's particular head size.

Wool knit cap (Jeep cap) which was often worn under the M1 helmet.

Cap, Field, Pile and Cap, Winter, OD; Tanker Bibs

Field pile cap used by the 10th Mountain Division.

Field pile cap label.

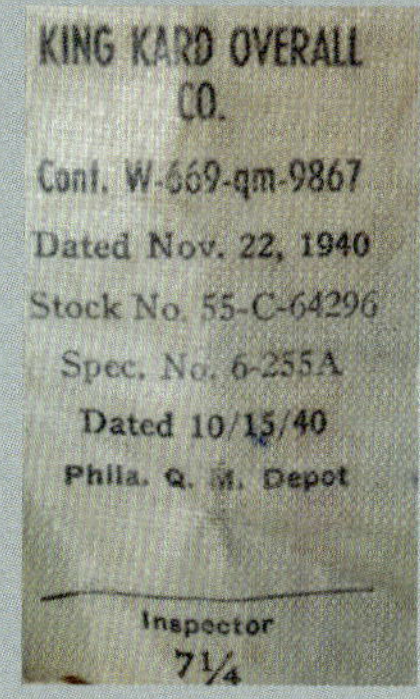

Inspection tag attached to sweatband of 1940 pattern "Cap, Winter, OD," shown below.

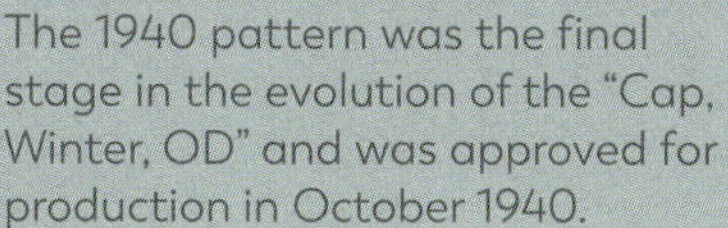

"Cap, Field, Pile, Olive Drab" with fur-covered visor. An officer's eagle was often attached to the front.

The 1940 pattern was the final stage in the evolution of the "Cap, Winter, OD" and was approved for production in October 1940.

Soldiers, probably from the 7th Service Command at Camp Hale, wearing the "Cap, Winter, OD." (John Adams-Graf)

10th Mountain Cavalry Reconnaissance Troop observer, February 6, 1945. The camp was about 4 mi. north of Maresca, Italy. The cavalry trooper is wearing the field pile cap and what appears to be tanker bibs. Tanker bibs were well-insulated overalls for tank crewmembers. Most American tanks had the engine in the rear with cooling fans blowing out the back. This resulted in a draft of cold air entering the driver and assistant driver's compartment and the turret. Consequently, the bibs were well insulated, warm, and needed. (John Adams-Graf)

Tanker bibs were wool-lined and made of cotton outer fabric, making them very warm.

Ski Caps

The 1942 first-pattern olive-drab cotton poplin ski cap has an olive-drab woolen flannel lining turned ear cape, with an adjustable chinstrap that pivots on its attachment points, and olive poplin-covered reinforced visor. This one is ink-stamped size "6 7/8" on the cotton sweatband. (John Adams-Graf)

The first-pattern ski cap is made of olive-drab cotton poplin. The earflaps drop down to cover the ears and the back of the head. The buckle chinstrap is secured by a rivet which allows strap adjustment. 10th Mountain veteran John Woodward models the cap.

The second-pattern ski cap was adopted for use by the 10th Mountain Division with interior earflaps that folded down to cover the wearer's ears. This ski cap is often confused with the ubiquitous Model 1943 Field Cap. It is easy to recognize the ski cap by the three seams that run from the back across the top of the cap to the visor. Markings include an ink-stamped size "6¾" and 1943-dated Seattle Cap & Apparel Mfg. Co. tag under the earflap. (John Adams-Graf)

Gaiters

Tweedie gaiter fastened to a ski boot.

"Medium U. S. Tweedie" imprinted on the inside.

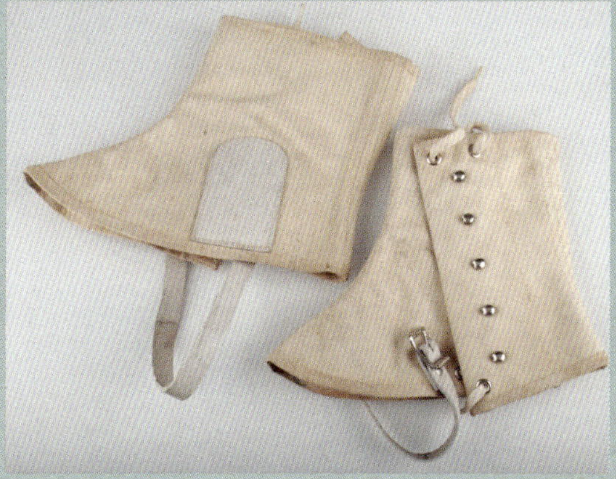
Short, white canvas second-pattern gaiters with light-white leather arch straps and laces, contract marked "L / U.S. / HOOD RUBBER CO., Inc. 1942." Although white gear is supposed to blend in with the snow, it would often get soiled and was easily spotted in snowy conditions.

Light-olive-drab short canvas gaiters with light-green leather arch straps and laces, contract marked "MEDIUM / U.S. / FINKLE UMBRELLA FRAME CO., INC." (John Adams-Graf)

Imprint on the olive-drab ski gaiter. (John Adams-Graf)

Imprint on the side of the white gaiter.

First-pattern ski gaiter with "Camp Hale" imprinted on the inside. (Harris)

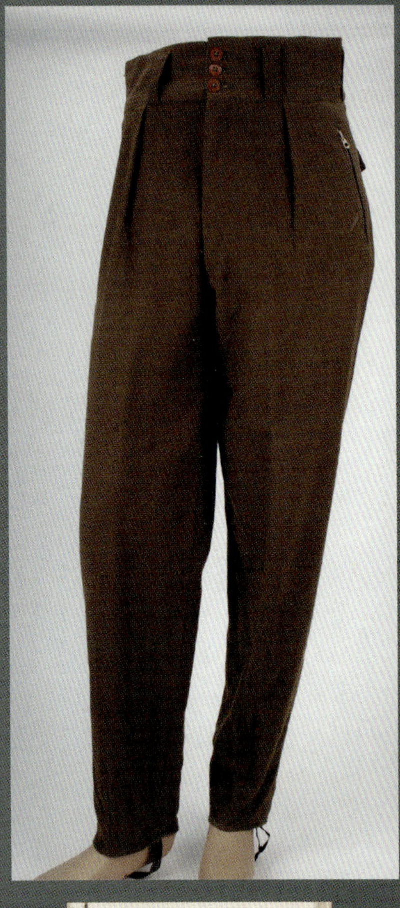

Pants

These olive-drab wool enlisted-issue ski trousers have a contract tag with size "32 × 31" and an April 7, 1942 date, with pleated front, inset rear pockets with button flaps, side pockets with zipper closures, three-button waistband closure, zipper fly, and pegged ankles with black elastic foot straps. (John Adams-Graf)

Ski trousers made of tough, water-repellant fabric with large cargo pockets on the side, and ordinary pockets that close with zippers and flaps. Dated Oct. 24, 1942. (John Adams-Graf)

A. L. KORNMAN CO.
Cont. W-669-qm-17236
Dated April 7, 1942
Stock No. 55-T-41253
32x31
Q. M. C. Tent. Spec.
P. Q. D. No. 75
Dated 6/23/41
Phila. Q. M. Depot

Inspection tag for wool ski trousers shown above. (John Adams-Graf)

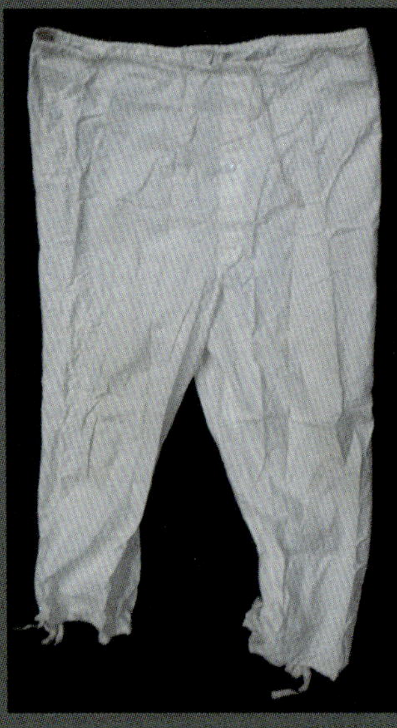

White camouflage over-pants.

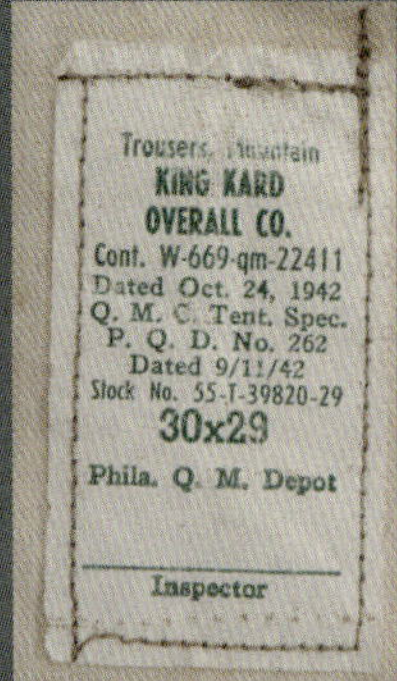

Inspection tag for water repellant trousers. (John Adams-Graf)

Parkas and Jackets

Overcoat parka with pile liner. Reversible OD to white cotton poplin knee-length parka with hood, large waist-level cargo pockets, and small inset slanted upper pockets. The white side shows staff sergeant chevrons. OD and ivory buttons are used throughout. (John Adams-Graf)

Parka, "Wet Weather, Construction 'A.'" Made by Climatic Rainwear Company, Inc., dated June 20, 1944. (John Adams-Graf)

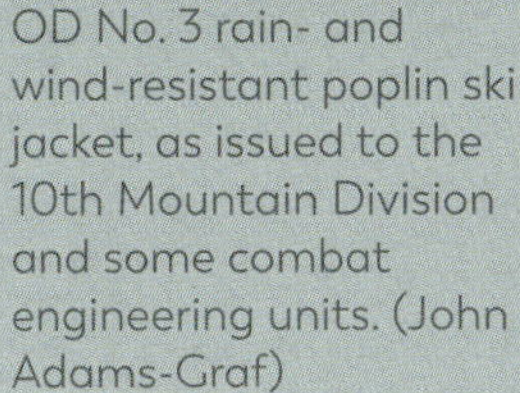

OD No. 3 rain- and wind-resistant poplin ski jacket, as issued to the 10th Mountain Division and some combat engineering units. (John Adams-Graf)

A Signal Corps photo with the caption "Hard working litter bearers of the 1st Bn., 80th Mtn. Inf., 10th Mtn. Div., contrast sharply against the cloudless sky along the crest of Mt. Belvedere while evacuating wounded infantrymen who stormed the strongly defended mountain." The bearers are wearing standard-issue M1943 field jackets, not the mountain jackets. (Signal Corps)

The design of the Army field jacket started with the 1939 pattern, the M1939 service coat, a long, woolen all-purpose coat. The next design was the M41 field jacket, which was lightweight and made of poplin with a woolen liner. It was found to be too lightweight and had insufficient pockets to carry items such as ammunition clips. The final version of the field jacket was the M43 jacket, as shown here. It had more pockets, was lightweight, acted as a windbreak, and could be worn over various layers of clothing.

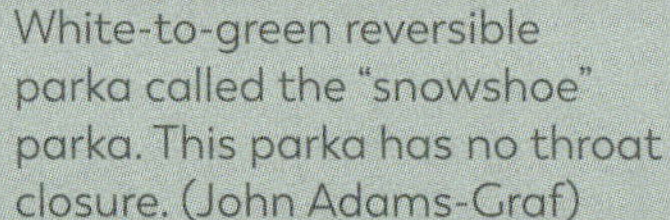

White-to-green reversible parka called the "snowshoe" parka. This parka has no throat closure. (John Adams-Graf)

First-pattern white-to-green reversible ski parka. This parka had a zippered throat closure. (John Adams-Graf)

Mountain and 1st Special Service Force troopers used the second-pattern white-to-green reversible parka with a fur-trimmed hood and buttoned slant pockets. The third-pattern, knee-length reversible parka added a drawstring at the hem and eliminated the fur around the cuffs. It had a buttoned throat closure. The 1942-dated contractor tag indicates size "MEDIUM." Whereas these were most often associated with Mountain and 1SSF troopers, these third-pattern parkas were also issued to infantry troops in Europe as stocks became available during the winter of 1944/45. (John Adams-Graf)

10th Mountain soldiers wearing second-pattern parkas and a snowshoe parka. (John Adams-Graf)

Shirts

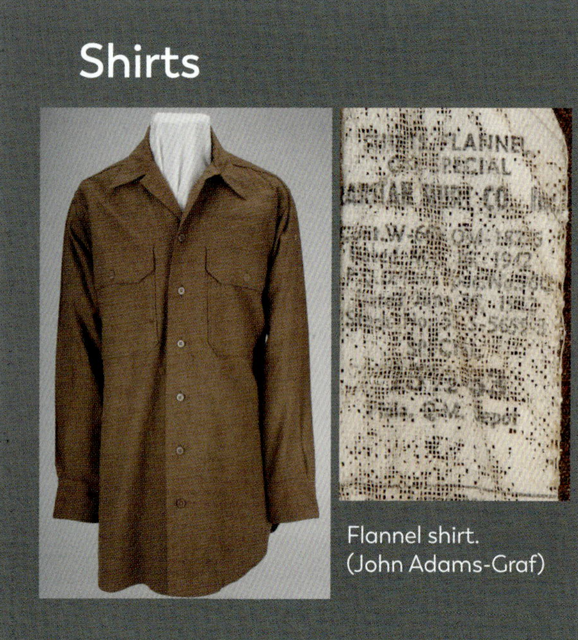

Flannel shirt. (John Adams-Graf)

Lightweight Jacket

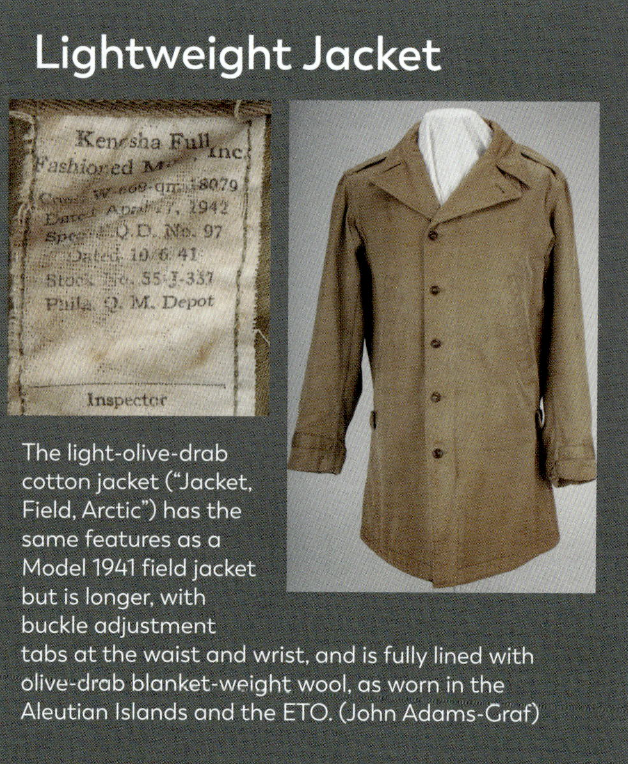

The light-olive-drab cotton jacket ("Jacket, Field, Arctic") has the same features as a Model 1941 field jacket but is longer, with buckle adjustment tabs at the waist and wrist, and is fully lined with olive-drab blanket-weight wool, as worn in the Aleutian Islands and the ETO. (John Adams-Graf)

Goggles

"Goggles, Ski-Mountain 1943 Type II" Foster Grant army-issue ski goggles with elastic band. The leather nosepiece is marked "F.G. Co."

First-pattern ski goggles. (Harris)

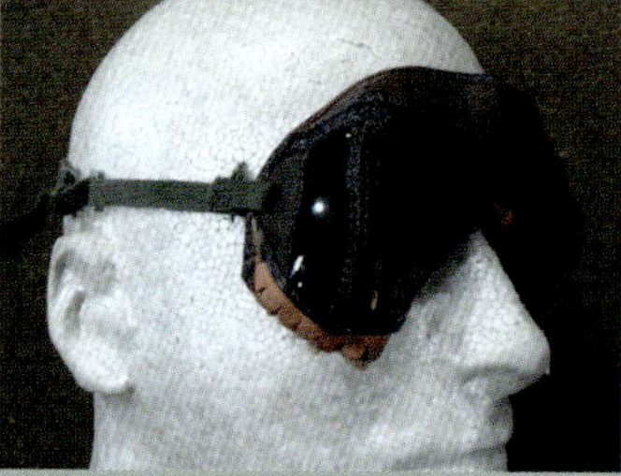

M-1943 Type III green-tinted Polaroid goggles as issued in 1943-dated paper case. Used by a wide variety of troops including 10th Mountain Division, tankers, machine-gunners, and paratroopers. These goggles have plastic lenses of three different shades.

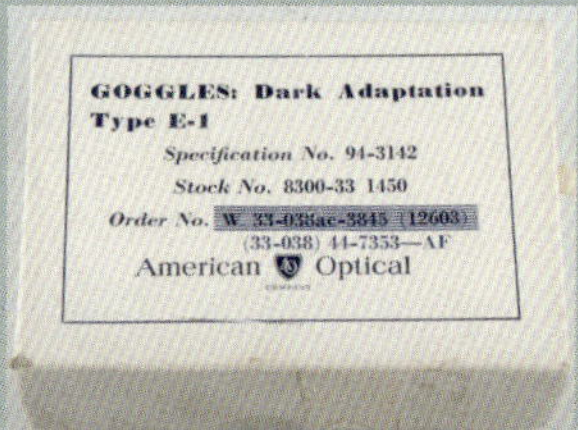

Box for Type E-1 goggles (not shown).

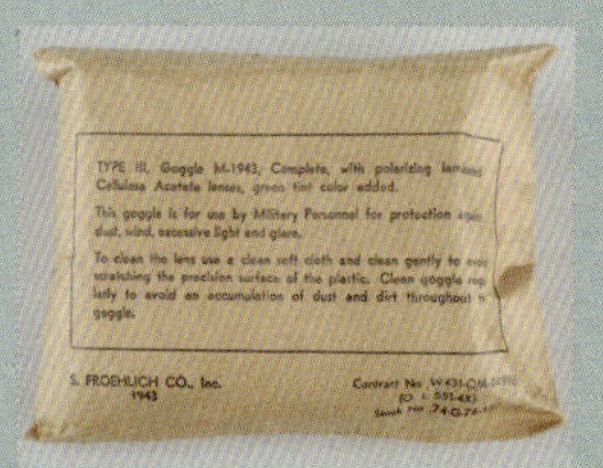

Paper packaging for M-1943 Type III goggles.

Socks and Suspenders

Woolen socks for ski boots. (John Adams-Graf)

Woolen socks for ski boots. These socks have a cushioned sole and are 60% wool and 40% cotton. The heels, toes, and soles of the socks are reinforced with wool. Ski boots were sized two sizes larger to accommodate layers of socks. (John Adams-Graf)

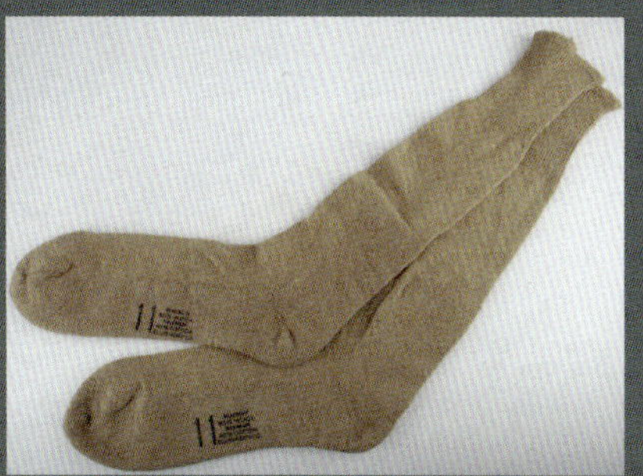

Jute hemp ski socks. (Harris)

A pair of unissued trouser suspenders with metal hooks designed for use with mountain trousers. (John Adams-Graf)

Mittens

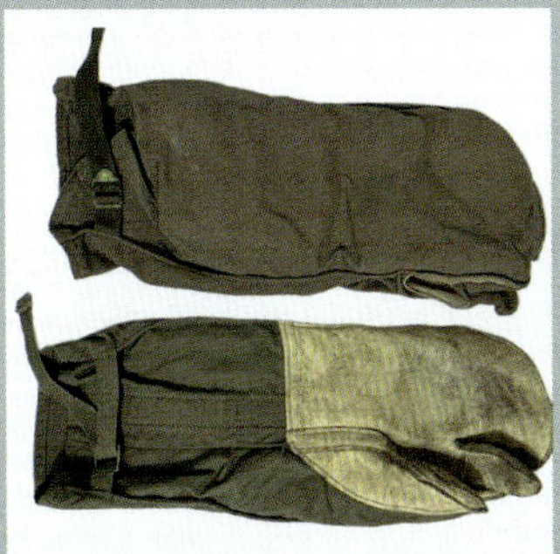

Wool-lined mitten with trigger finger. (Harris)

Liner for white mitten cover. The mitten is Type 1 with trigger finger. (John Adams-Graf)

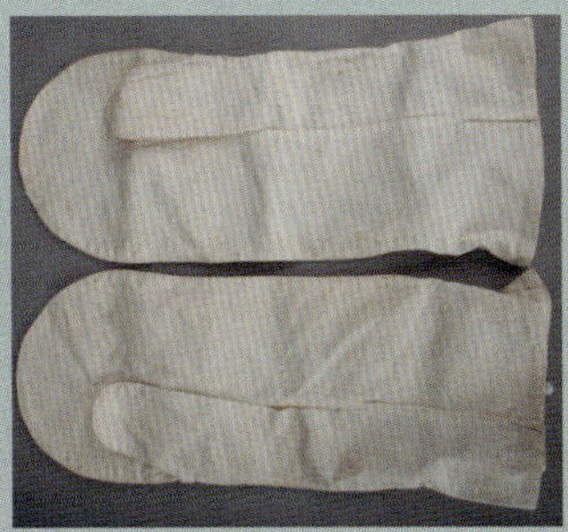

Matching pair of cotton "Mittens, Overwhite" made to be worn over the trigger finger mittens. A buttoned flap on the other side allows access to the trigger finger on the internal mitten. (John Adams-Graf)

Ski trooper wearing leather mittens and Polaroid commercial-pattern green-tinted goggles. (John Adams-Graf)

Boots

The M1944 design of cloth-topped four-buckle overshoes with rubber soles. These were designed to fit over the soldiers' shoes and were issued to units in areas where cold, wet conditions existed, but not to all units. (John Adams-Graf)

Shoe Pacs were leather boots with a rubber lower sole that were warm and quite effective in reducing water saturation. These boots reduced the chance of trench foot, and were used by the 10th in Kiska and in Italy.

"M1943 Combat Service Boots Double Buckle." Leggings were not necessary with these boots. These were used by the 10th in Italy.

These first-pattern M1938 leggings had nine hooks (left). The second pattern had eight hooks (middle). The USMC issue had six hooks (right).

U.S. Army service shoes, Blücher Pattern, ½ bellows tongue, full toe vamp, toecap without box toe and rubber sole.

Corporal John Graf wearing four-buckle overshoes at Camp Hale. (John Adams-Graf)

Leggings and service shoes of an MP unit at Camp Hale. From left: Earl Peterson, Ken Christopherson, and Frank Hopricnik. (John Adams-Graf)

Service shoe with M1938 second-pattern legging attached. The purpose of the legging was to allow lower-leg protection when using a lowcut service shoe, which saved leather compared to the two-buckle boot. The legging was manufactured from canvas material, which absorbed water and often chaffed the leg. It took a long time to secure the legging to the leg, often with difficulty. That is why the soldiers preferred the two-buckle boot, which did not require leggings.

Service Uniforms

The officer at far left is wearing a dark OD shade 51 service coat with tan trousers ("Pinks"). This uniform was often referred to as "Pinks and Greens." The tunic is worn with a khaki shade 1 shirt and khaki mohair tie. The Sam Browne belt was optional after 1942. The three enlisted men are wearing the M1939 four-pocket wool service coat in OD shade 54. The 10th ski trooper, second from the right, is wearing woolen trousers in OD shade 54. The trooper second from the left wears light-shade OD trousers. The two enlisted men in the front row are wearing white gaiters over ski/hiking boots. White gaiters, ski boots, woolen ski trousers, and service caps were authorized for the Class A uniform. The WAC to the right is wearing a dark OD shade 51 tunic with the officer's skirt, wool, drab, light shade.

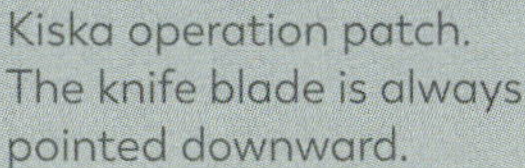

Kiska operation patch. The knife blade is always pointed downward.

10th Mountain Division patch and Mountain rocker.

Officer's winter service uniform, called the "Chocolate Brown," olive-drab shade 51 tunic. This example is a full-length officer's tunic with first lieutenant rank. On the left shoulder is the 10th Mountain Division patch, while on the right is the Kiska operation patch. The uniform has an attached belt, which replaced the leather Sam Browne belt from World War I.

World War II veteran Sergeant Jim Keck (85th Inf.) wearing dark OD shade 51 tunic, khaki shirt with black tie.

Male officer's overseas cap, shade 51 olive drab.

Contrasting tan trousers, often called "Pinks," to go with the chocolate-brown tunic. Brown reproduction shoes are also shown.

7th Service Command patch used by service units at Camp Hale.

John Graf, member of the 7th Service Command MP Detachment at Camp Hale. Notice the seven-point 7th Service Command patch. (John Adams-Graf)

Women's chocolate-brown officer's tunic, winter service uniform with Army Service Forces shoulder patch, and WAC second lieutenant rank. There was a WAC detachment at Camp Hale from the 7th Service Command.

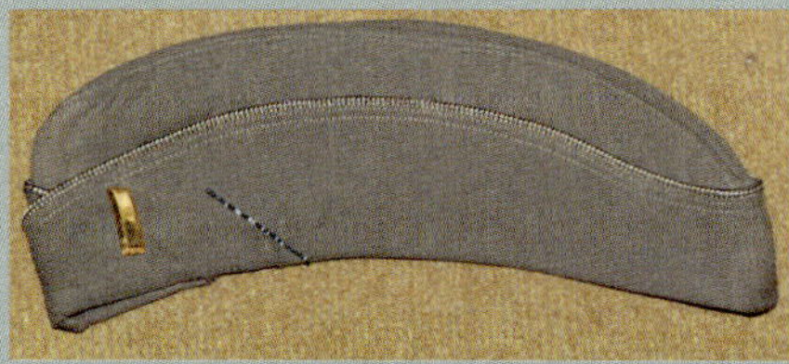

Women's chocolate-brown service cap.

Women's chocolate-brown winter service tunic with light-shade woolen skirt.

Women's chocolate-brown winter service tunic with matching skirt.

Men and women officers' summer Class A khaki tunic uniforms.

Officer's summer service uniforms.

Officer's khaki cap and tie.

"Waist, Wool, Women's" lightweight woolen flannel shirt.

Field Uniforms

Class B enlisted field uniform.

Women's coverall fatigue uniform, herringbone twill pattern (HBT).

A lieutenant from the 10th Mountain Division wearing herringbone twill coveralls. (John Adams-Graf)

HBT weave pattern for fatigues.

Equipment for Movement over Snow

The 10th Mountain Division had unique mountaineering duties. One of those was to travel over snow and attack the enemy. The division was equipped with skis, skiing equipment, and snowshoes to perform these tasks. This chapter deals with the snow skis, ski bindings, ski boots, ski poles, climbing skins, snowshoes, and skiing techniques required for handling a heavy backpack.

Ski trooper reenactor skiing with original 10th Mountain Division equipment.

Snow Skis

Several manufacturers made snow skis for the 10th Mountain Division, including Northland, Groswold, Paris, and Artek-Roscoe. The skis were approximately 7 ft. long and made of steam-bent hickory with steel edges. In 1945, laminated skis were introduced which allowed the ski to be flexible and formed the ski's reverse camber needed for making turns. The segmented steel edges were a relatively advanced feature for commercial military skis. They could grip hard-pack snow and not wear out like skis with the customary wooden edge. Early versions of the skis were very stiff and had to be shaved down a little on the top deck to make them more flexible.

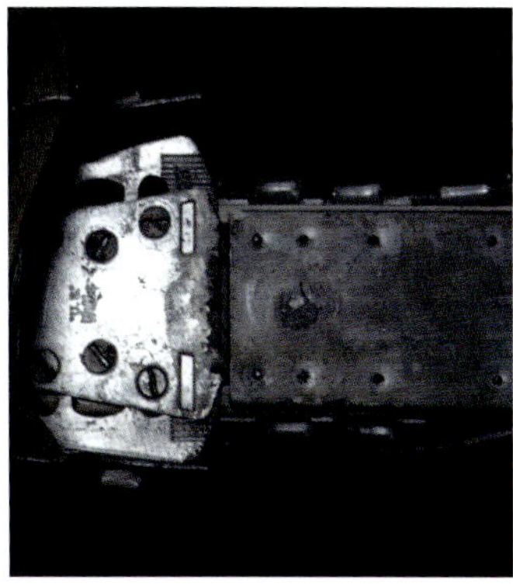

Ski-binding toe lug showing the manufacturer as "Wilby."

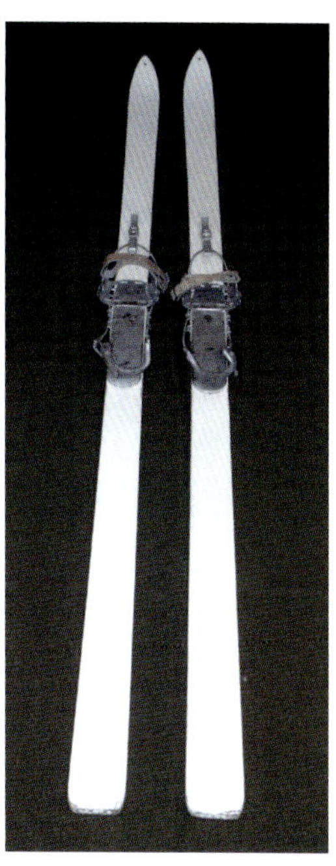

A pair of 10th Mountain skis viewed from the tail. The skis were approximately 7 ft. long with minimal sidecut. Bindings were placed slightly aft of the middle of the skis. The holes at the tip were called rescue holes that allowed two skis to be attached to form a rescue sled to transport an injured soldier. All skis were painted white to blend in with the snow environment. Skis were fitted to ski troopers by having the soldier reach with an arm as high as possible and measure the distance from the tip of the fingers to the floor. Since the front toepiece of the binding was fitted to a ski boot, the result was a left and right ski.

The number engraved near the toe binding on 10th Mountain Division skis is the date of manufacture. In this case, it reads 4-43, which is the fourth month of 1943.

The shovel or ski tip of a typical 10th Mountain Division ski. The rescue hole for connecting the skis to make a sled is visible.

The bottom of a ski tip with the manufacturer engraved "Northland Skis, St. Paul, Minnesota." All skis for the military had "U.S." as part of the engraving.

The bottom of the ski. The wood was hickory with multiple laminations for flexibility. The steel edges were secured by screws which would occasionally back out and were usually checked and retightened by the ski trooper. If a screw stuck out after tightening, then the trooper typically filed it flat. The center groove on the bottom of the ski helped keep the ski tracking when sliding forward. Folding skis were tested but were not sufficiently rigid to support a skier and were not adopted.

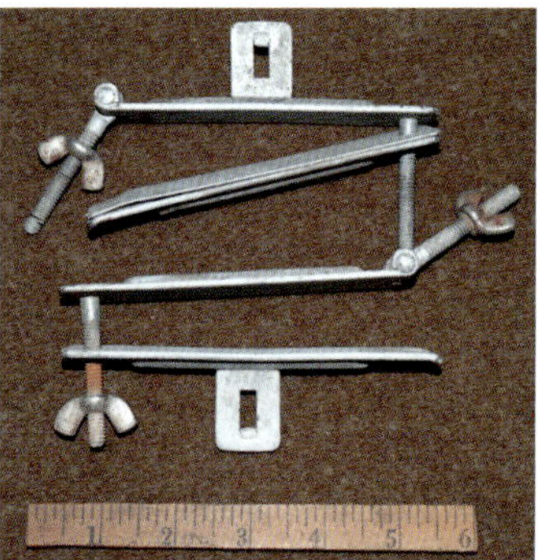

Small ski rack to secure skis to a Weasel or other vehicle.

A 10th Mountain trooper reenacts with the original equipment. The pack is secured with shoulder straps and a belly strap. The rifle is attached via a clip at the bottom sling fitting and a strap attached to the backpack.

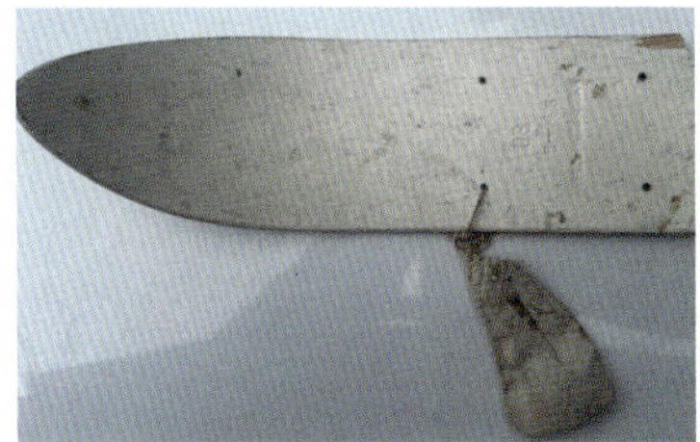

Breaking a ski tip in high-country deep or ungroomed snow was not unusual. A temporary replacement ski tip could be screwed to the original fractured ski tip. This would simulate an intact ski tip, and the skier could return to base with minimal difficulty. (Little)

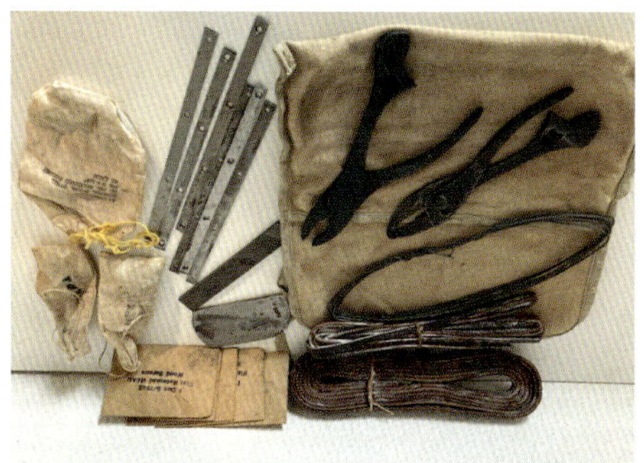

Ski repair kit that includes segmented edges, mounting screws, leather strap material, and tools for repairing skis in the field. (Harris)

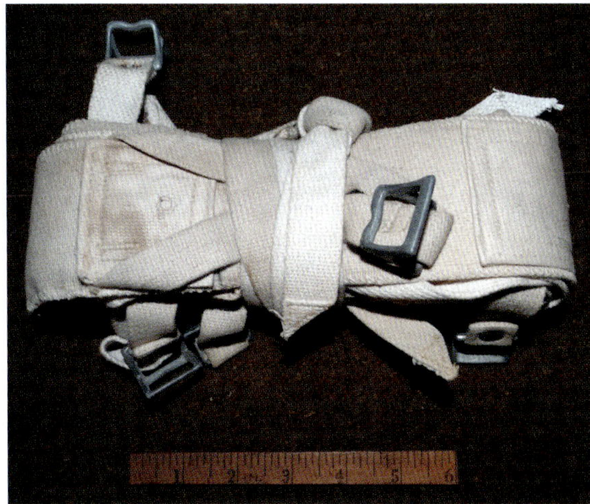

Climbers were synthethic mohair fabric strips worn on the bottom of the skis to prevent back sliding when climbing steep snow slopes. Climbers were issued in different lengths to accommodate various ski sizes. These were approximately 77 in. long. Climbers were often called seal skins. In some instances, with heavy 90 lb. backpacks, soldiers used climbers to descend a slope and keep from sliding too fast with such a load. Shown here are military climbers wrapped up.

Here are the civilian climbers (in the natural darker color of the animal's fur that was used to make the seal skins) and the white mohair military climbers. Early in the war, 10th Mountain ski troopers used their own personal climbers until they were supplied with the military version.

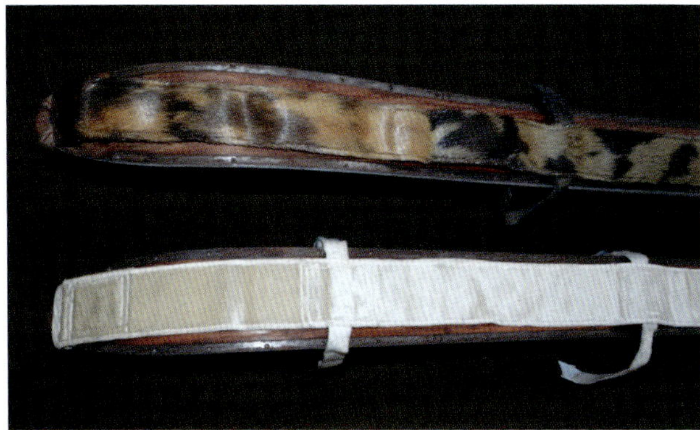

The installation of U.S. Army synthetic mohair climbing skins and the civilian climbing skins in natural-colored fur. The skin was fitted over the ski tip, and the straps along the length secured the climbing skin to the bottom of the ski.

The Universal Stay Co. was a manufacturer of U.S. Army climbing skins.

Ski Wax

Blue ski wax for dry snow. Waxes were either animal fat, pitch, or rosin, used as ski wax to waterproof skis. These waxes were used to protect wooden skis from water absorption. An unintended benefit was that these substances are hydrophobic, which repelled water, reduced friction between the ski and snow, and made it glide more easily. (John Adams-Graf)

Waxes for various snow conditions, such as wet and corn snow, dry snow, and granular snow. Later in the war, tubes were made of cardboard to save on materials.

Ski Boots

The U.S. Army ski and mountain boots were developed from civilian ski boots that needed an upgrade for military usage. The civilian ski boot had a square toe that fitted the typical Kandahar ski-binding design at the time. The boot also had a groove in the heel to accept the heel cable from the binding. The military version had similar characteristics but was beefed up with thicker leather and a heavier sole. The U.S. Army developed four basic patterns of the ski boot. The first ski boot pattern was adopted under Tentative Specification BQD31. This boot had a smooth leather sole and a foam-padded tongue. It was close in appearance to civilian ski boots at that time and was designated "Boot, Ski." The second pattern of the military ski boot was developed under Tentative Specification BQD31A, designated "Boot, Mountain, and Ski." The boot had a large vamp that covered the toe box and six lines of stitching near the toe. Some deficiencies existed with this pattern, so a third pattern was developed under Tentative Specification BQD31B.

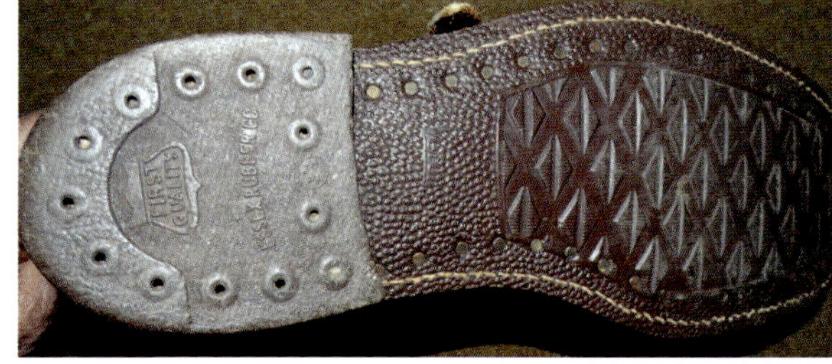

Typical civilian ski boot from the 1930s.

Tentative Specification BQD31A, May 12, 1942, introduced the high box toe typical of World War II army ski boots. These boots are recognizable from the distinctive three-piece tongue made of leather, smooth soles, and six lines of stitching on the toe box. The boot had metal-tipped white shoelaces. It had many flaws because of a lack of testing and was the basis for the redesigned boot BQD31B. (John Adams-Graf)

Soles of BQD31A marked "U.S.A. / No. 75 / E / 8½." (John Adams-Graf)

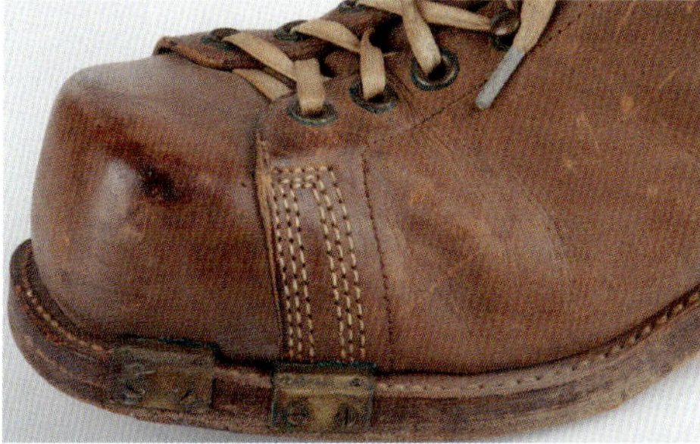

The six lines of stitching on the toe box. (John Adams-Graf)

Boot with steel (Tricouni) cleats to enhance climbing on slick surfaces. Cleats could be ordered separately from the quartermaster and installed on a ski boot.

Early war model ski boot Tentative Specification BQD31B with a woolen felt insole.

The third pattern featured smooth leather soles and a rubber heel insert. The toe box leather was extended toward the heel, eliminating a forward-facing seam and the six lines of stitching. The boot also had a toe spring, which is the upward angle of the toe and aids in walking. The third-pattern boot was produced in two versions: smooth soles for fitting in a ski binding and mountain boots with cleats—the Tricouni nails. The third pattern was designated "Boot, Ski-Mountain" and "Boot, Ski-Mountain with Nails." Having two sets of boots for each soldier was considered impractical, so a fourth pattern was developed under Tentative Specification BQD31C, which was designated "Boot, Ski-Mountain with Rubber Cleated Sole." This was the final ski/mountain boot design with a rubber cleated sole that worked well for climbing and was compatible with ski bindings. The rubber sole version was quieter than those made of leather when climbing on rocky terrain. The size marked on the boots assumed the soldier was wearing heavy socks and was two sizes larger than the soldier's barefoot size. Without the heavy socks, size 8 ski/mountain boots would fit a soldier who typically wore size 10 shoes. The ankle-high boot and bear-trap bindings made soldiers' ankles vulnerable to injury during falls while skiing.

Final version of 10th Mountain Division ski boots, Tentative Specification BQD31C, September 1943. This boot was a combination ski/mountain boot with toe protectors, a heel groove for skiing, and a heavy tread for mountain climbing. U.S. Army ski boots have a sole shaped like a rocker (toe spring) for ease in walking and climbing. Goodyear received a temporary patent after the war and sold the "Goodyear Vibram Lug Sole," the most popular climbing/combat sole, for over 75 years. The patent reverted to the Vibramani Company in Italy 50 years after the end of the war.

The Goodyear Rubber Company manufactured this boot sole.

The A. E. Nettleton Company, founded in 1879 by A. E. Nettleton in Syracuse, New York, and known for producing high-end gentlemen's footwear, was a manufacturer of the fourth-pattern ski boot.

Fourth-pattern ski boots.

Ski Bindings

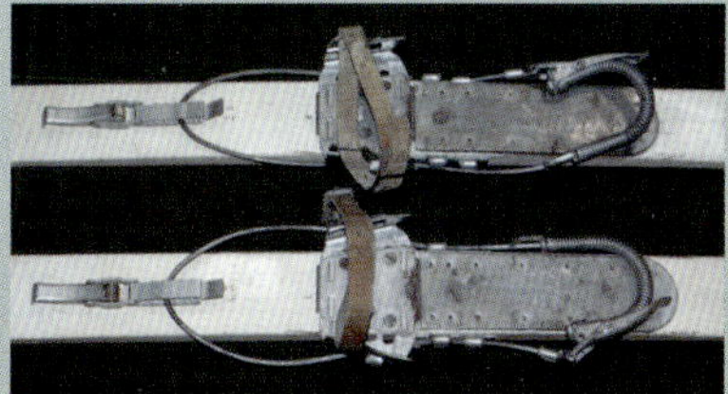

Typical Kandahar bindings—named after the Kandahar Ski Club in 1929—used by 10th Mountain Division soldiers. The boot toe fitted in the binding toepiece.

Kandahar binding with heel cable fitted through both grips on the ski side guides for downhill skiing. The heel was clamped to the ski, facilitating steering of the skis when using the snowplow and Stem Christie techniques.

The heel cable passing through only the forward grip on the Kandahar binding allowed the heel of the ski boot to lift, making it easier to cross-country ski.

A runaway strap was connected from the binding to a location on the shoe or shoelace to prevent the skis from taking off if the binding released.

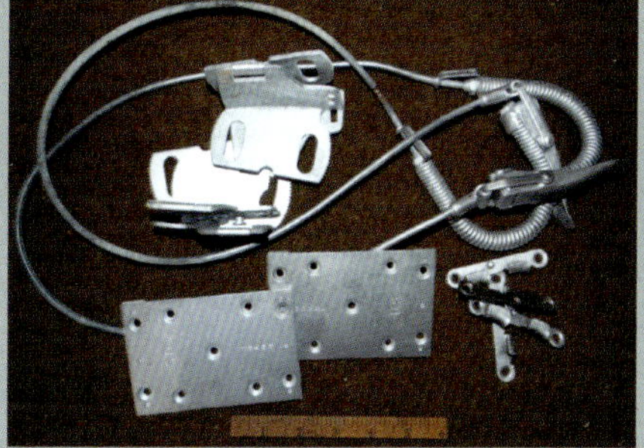

Kandahar bindings manufactured by Dovre Ski Binding Company as delivered in a box with all parts, including mounting screws. Leif Nashe and Odd Overgaard started the Dovre Ski Binding Company.

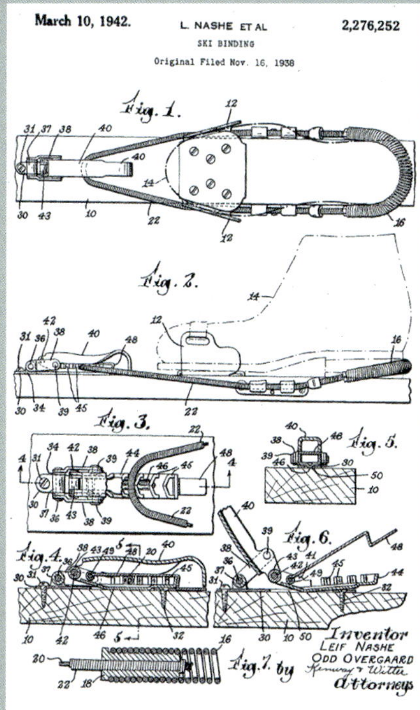

U.S. utility patent by Leif Nashe and Odd Overgaard showing the concept of their Kandahar-style ski binding.

Dovre ski-binding ski boot plate.

Printing on the side of a box containing a pair of Dovre ski bindings.

Ski Poles

Ski pole basket manufactured by Northland Ski Company. The basket prevents the ski pole from being planted too deep in the snow. A tanned leather lattice supports the wooden molded ring and is connected to the ski pole with a cotter pin.

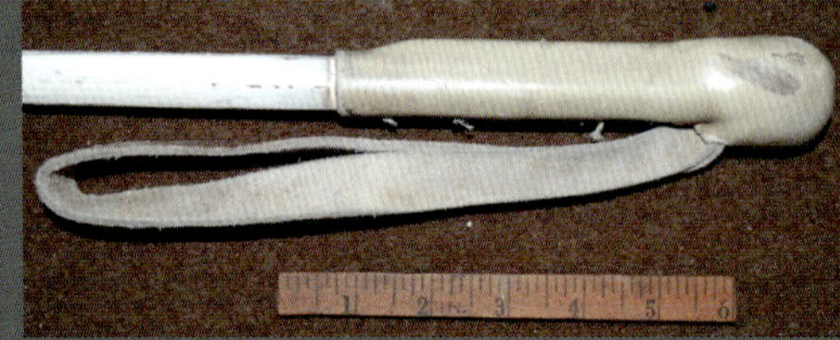

Northland ski pole grip with hand strap.

Identifying mark on Northland ski pole tip.

Northland six-sided ski pole made from bamboo.

Identifying mark on ski pole tip manufactured by Montague Ski Company.

Montague ski pole grip with hand strap.

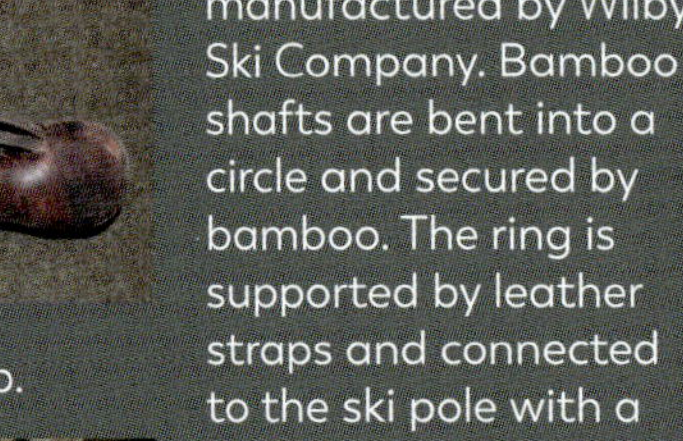

Ski pole basket manufactured by Wilby Ski Company. Bamboo shafts are bent into a circle and secured by bamboo. The ring is supported by leather straps and connected to the ski pole with a cotter pin.

Identifying mark on Wilby ski pole tip.

Wilby ski pole grip and leather strap.

Ski pole basket for an aluminum ski pole. The aluminum ring is supported by a leather lattice and connected to the ski pole with a cotter pin.

Aluminum ski pole grip and leather strap.

Snowshoes

C. A. Lund Bear-paw snowshoes for the U.S. Army. The size is 13 in. by 28 in.

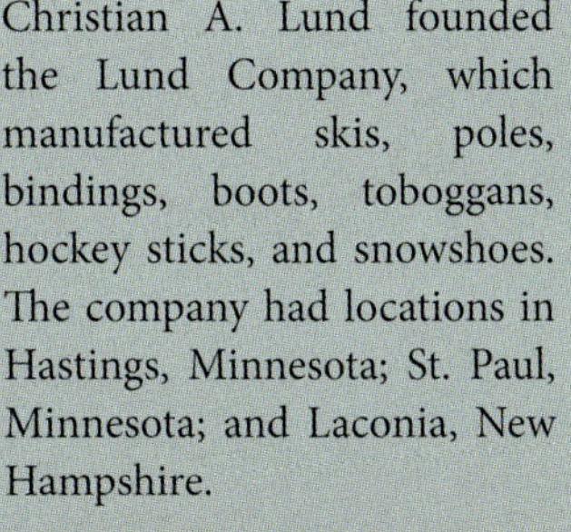

Christian A. Lund founded the Lund Company, which manufactured skis, poles, bindings, boots, toboggans, hockey sticks, and snowshoes. The company had locations in Hastings, Minnesota; St. Paul, Minnesota; and Laconia, New Hampshire.

Engraving by C. A. Lund Company for the U.S. Army.

Ski trooper reenactor with Bear-paw snowshoes.

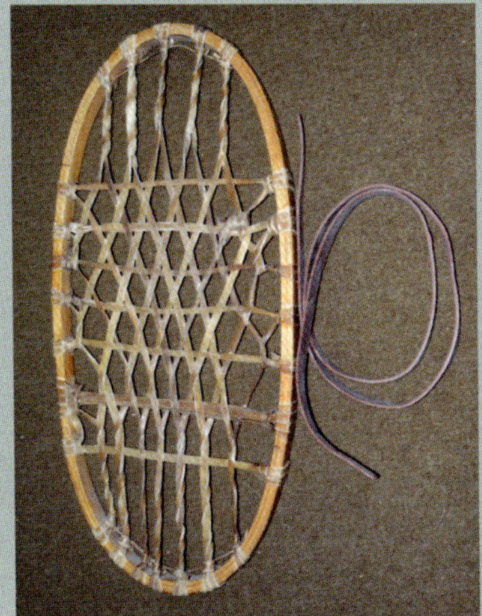

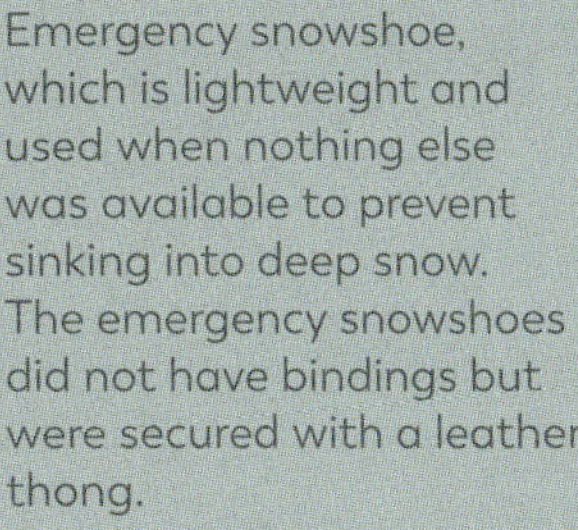

Emergency snowshoe, which is lightweight and used when nothing else was available to prevent sinking into deep snow. The emergency snowshoes did not have bindings but were secured with a leather thong.

The serial number and the dimensions of the emergency snowshoe in inches.

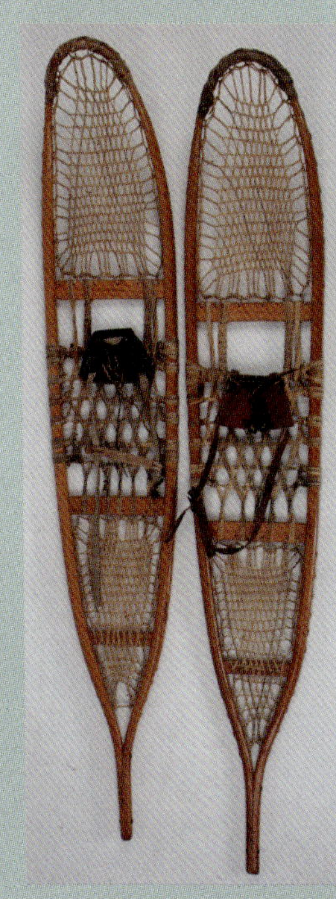

Trail snowshoes made by the A & F. H. Company (Abercrombie & Fitch Holding) of Wallingford, Vermont, one of four companies producing snowshoes for the war. Their dimensions are 10 in. by 58 in. They are also date-stamped. During the war and in training, snowshoes were simply tossed into a pile for the supply sergeant to put away. Usually, this meant that pairs were not matched with their original numbers. The snowshoes have their original leather bindings.

Binding attached to trail snowshoe.

Abercrombie & Fitch Holding, manufacturer of this trail snowshoe.

Trail snowshoe binding.

Johnson-Carper Furniture Co., the manufacturer of the toboggan. (Little)

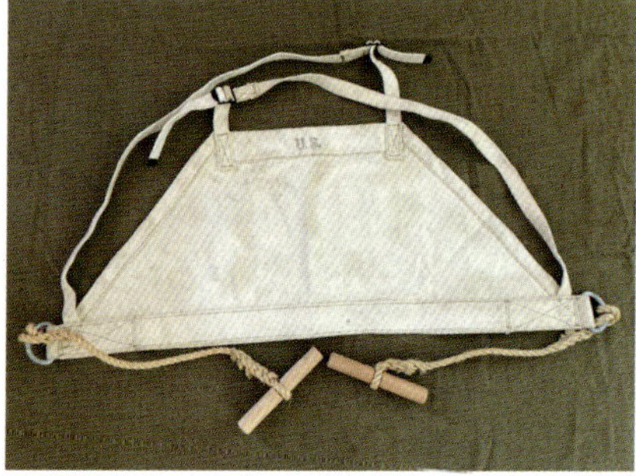

"Harness, Man, Two Trace Apron" used for pulling a toboggan. (Harris)

Putting on trail snowshoes in Italy, in front of an M10 tank destroyer, 1945. (John Adams-Graf)

Topside view of a 10th Mountain Division toboggan. (Little)

Trail snowshoes in use at Camp Hale. (John Adams-Graf)

The 10th Mountain Division Skiing Technique of World War II

During World War II, the 10th Mountain Division was formed to act as the mountain troop contingent of the U.S. Army due to the efforts of Charles Minot Dole (founder of the National Ski Patrol in 1938). Skiers from all over the country were invited to join the 10th if they had three letters of recommendation recognized by the existing hierarchy of the 10th. Lieutenant John Woodward, Pacific Northwest Intercollegiate Champion in 1936 and future U.S. Ski and Snowboard Hall of Fame member, joined the military in the 15th Infantry, leading the ski patrol in that unit. Shortly afterward, he was assigned to the 10th Light Division and was made the head ski instructor at the 10th. Later, in 1944, the 10th Light Division became the 10th Mountain Division, and Woodward was assigned to the 87th Infantry Regiment. His duty was to train ski instructors and develop a teaching progression for U.S. Army ski troops.

Ski trooper reenactor with rifle and rucksack weighing approximately 90 lb.

The instruction progression included walking on skis, the sidestep, the herringbone, climbing with seal skins, the snowplow turn, the stem turn, the lifted stem turn, and the parallel turn. When skiers get together to discuss skiing, disagreements may arise about how to ski. According to Woodward, disputes regarding ski technique in the 10th Mountain Division were settled by referring to the "Skier's Bible," a book entitled *Downhill Skiing* by Otto Lang. The methodology in the Lang's book appeared to work with ski troops unencumbered by heavy equipment. However, as the 10th Mountain Division progressed toward a fighting-ready division, the amount of equipment required to be carried by a ski trooper often exceeded 90 lb. This included an M1 Garand rifle (an additional 9½ lb.) and a rucksack carrying ammunition, tools, camping gear, and clothing.

Dealing with such a heavy rucksack significantly affected the ski technique used by the 10th. Simply traversing on skis was a chore with this load. A wide track stance was necessary to stabilize the weight. One ski settling more into soft snow could cause a weight shift that would result in a fall due to an unrecoverable loss of balance. 10th veteran Gordon (Tiny) McQuade weighed slightly less than 100 lb. during his training in 1943. He recounted that he could not get up when he fell on his skis while lugging a rucksack, and two fellow troopers had to lift him. His dislike of the 90 lb. pack was so intense that on an occasional day training outing, he would stuff his pack full of pillows to make it appear that he was carrying a fully loaded pack. This worked for a while until his sergeant discovered his ploy. He was immediately sent to KP (kitchen patrol) duty peeling potatoes, punishment for wayward troops.

Platoon Sergeant Hugh Evans was an experienced skier when he joined the 10th Mountain Division. He found it very difficult to ski with the 90 lb. pack. Fresh recruits had a greater problem since they would cross-country ski about 100 yd. and fall over. It took another trooper to lift off their pack and get them up. The secret with the 90 lb. pack was to ski slowly. The soldiers typically froze seal skins to the bottom of the skis to increase friction, so the skis skied slowly. All turns were typically snowplow and stem turns. Traveling at speed downhill with the 90 lb. pack was unusual, so very few photos of such an endeavor exist. Skis were used primarily for transportation, to get across the snow to the next objective with all the equipment.

29. Stem Christiania.

a. The stem christiania (fig. 50) is the most advanced turn to be learned by the soldier. It is a good turn in both soft snow and hard snow, on steep or gradual slopes, and can be used at moderate speed or high speed.

b. To start the turn more speed is necessary than with the stem turn. The counterstem is made with

Figure 50. Stem christiania.

195

U.S. Army Field Manual. (FM 70-15)

Stem turn with a quiet upper body.

The November 1944 field manual put forth by the War Department gave little guidance on how to ski with a heavy rucksack. In 1942, there was no field manual for skiers, so the cadre at the 10th Mountain Division utilized Lang's book. In 1944, an Army manual was developed providing guidance on how to perform the Stem Christiania (Christie) and other turns. The skiing technique in the Army Field Manual was identical to that described in Lang's book. The Stem Christie entailed a counter-rotation of the upper body at turn initiation, followed by upper-body rotation through the turn. This technique worked for the skier without a loaded rucksack. However, when the ski troops tried this, the rotation, coupled with the increased inertia of the 90 lb. rucksack and rifle, caused instability as it rotated and counter-rotated with the upper body. The rifle buttstock was attached to the pack with a clip, while the grip near the barrel used a web belt to secure it to the top of the pack. The rifle often shifted back and forth with this arrangement, adding to a higher center of mass and random load movement, resulting in extreme difficulty while skiing with the fully loaded rucksack. According to Woodward, the technique was modified by quieting the upper body and eliminating the rotation and counter-rotation.

The above photograph shows a ski trooper performing a stem turn with the upper body following the direction of the skis without counter-rotation or rotation. More active twisting (steering) of the feet and the lower body was used to compensate for the loss of upper-body movement. This was difficult because of the flexibility of the early leather, ankle-high ski boots.

The 1943-vintage ski boots lacked the fore/aft and lateral stiffness of today's modern ski boot, making it difficult to maintain balance when negotiating steep slopes with a heavy load on the skier's back. Conversations with 10th veteran Robert Parker also shed light on the effect of the rucksack weight on the lifted stem turn. The lifted stem turn is performed by shifting all weight to the outside leg while the inside leg is lifted off the snow to a parallel position and then weighted. Care had to be taken while shifting weight with the 90 lb. rucksack by flexing the knees and ankles to keep the center of mass low and controllable. The lifting of the inside ski had to be rapid to quickly regain the wide parallel traverse stance at the end of the turn. The parallel ski position was hip-width, wide-track to form a stable base for the heavy combined weight of the skier and pack. A narrow-track, feet-together stance did not work out well since it made it easy to fall to one side or the other.

The Army never addressed skiing with a heavy rucksack and rifle. This was left to the soldiers of the 10th to do their best to modify the skiing technique of the time to accomplish their mission as "Soldiers on Skis."

The caption under this U.S. Army Signal Corps photo reads as follows: "Sgt. Stephen P. Knowlton, Durham, N.H., I & R Platoon, 86th Mountain Inf., 10th Mountain Div., does a couple of short turns to get his 'ski legs' as he prepares to leave on a three-day ski patrol deep into enemy territory." (Signal Corps)

Signal Corps photo with a caption that reads: "Hall Burton, mountain trooper, carrying a full pack and rifle, exhibits his skill on skis. Camp Hale, Colo." (Signal Corps)

Mountaineering Equipment

Specialized equipment used in the mountain environment and extremely cold conditions was provided to the 10th Mountain Division. This chapter reviews standard divisional equipment, and the equipment required for a mountain environment, including the mountain tent, piton equipment, glacier equipment, ice axes, cooking gear, backboards, and rucksacks.

Mountain Tent

The 10th Mountain Division two-man tent was lightweight and waterproof. It was reversible and could be set up with the white side out or the olive-drab side out. Since the tent was waterproof, it did not transmit moisture other than through the vents at each end of the tent. This resulted in excessive moisture accumulation inside the tent, making the moisture unbearable to many mountain troops. Some troops laid the tent on the snow, placed their sleeping bags on top, and slept on top of the tent. The tent was made of cotton fabric with a waterproofing nylon coating. Early versions of the tent had one entry, but later designs had an entry at both ends.

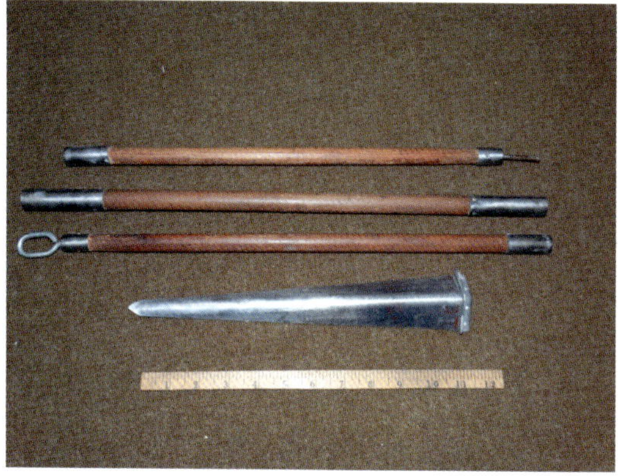

Tent poles and stakes for a 10th Mountain Division tent. The stake was made of aluminum to reduce weight. The tent poles were erected in pockets outside the tent since the tent had a floor.

Tent kit showing tent and poles.

Piton Hammer and Pitons

Wartime-issued 10th Mountain Division piton hammer (not to be confused with the all-green 1950s-issued hammer) with correct square steel head and a pointed "beak" on a 9 in. unpainted wooden handle. A long, white leather thong was tied to the handle to wear around the neck when climbing. The Ames Company manufactured most of the piton hammers. Other manufacturers made the hammers between 1944 and 1945 after the 10th received the Ames hammers. (John Adams-Graf)

View of hammer head from the side. (John Adams-Graf)

"NE US-45" stamped on the underside of the hammer. (John Adams-Graf)

Piton information. (OQMG Circular No. 4, August 1943)

SNAPLINKS, MOUNTAIN
Stock No. 74-S-295

A steel link used to attach the mountain climbing or holding rope to the pitons and to transmit strain from the rope to the piton in the event of a fall. These are made to withstand a pull of 2000 lbs. and can be easily manipulated with one hand.

Fig. 1—The Snaplink, Mountain
Figs. 2 and 3—Piton, Mountain, Type I, attached to the Snaplink

PITONS, MOUNTAIN

Fig. No.	Type	Stock No.
3	I	74-P-133-15
4	II	74-P-133-20
5	III	74-P-133-25
6	V	74-P-133-35
7	IV	74-P-133-30

FIG. 1

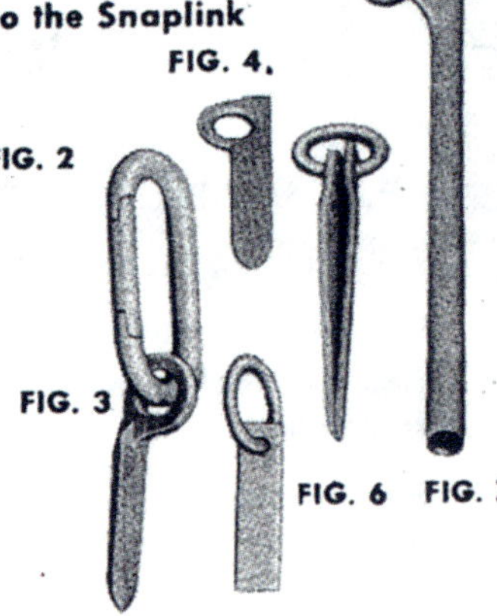

Pitons, types I, II, III, and V, are soft iron spikes which are driven into cracks of various width and shapes in the rock to provide security for men or equipment in operations involving steep rock ascents. Type IV, a hollow tube, may be driven into ice for the same purpose.

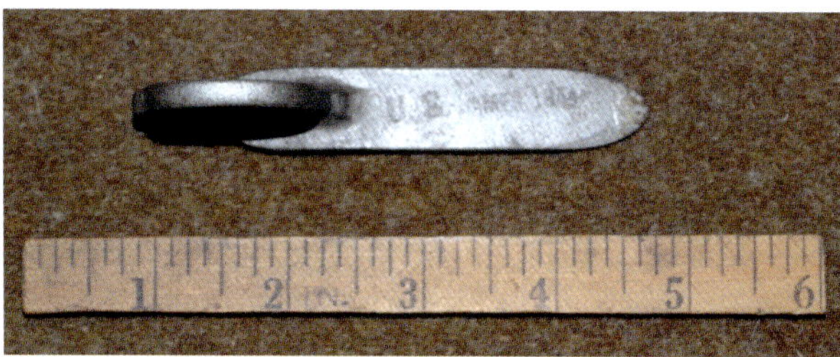

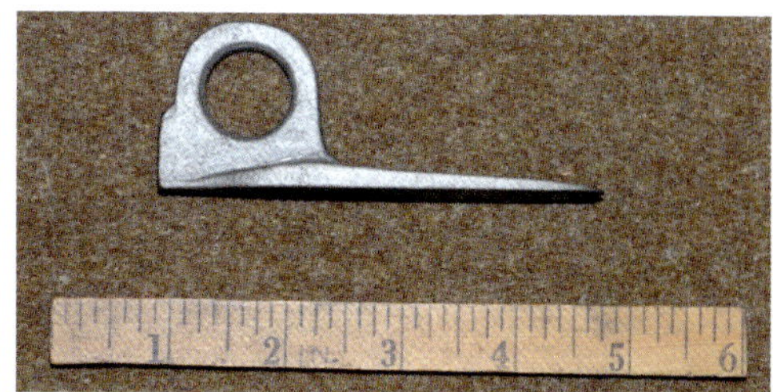

The Ames Corporation army pitons (1942–44). Manufacturer names were stamped into the piton until 1944, but later, the names were printed to avoid weakening the metal.

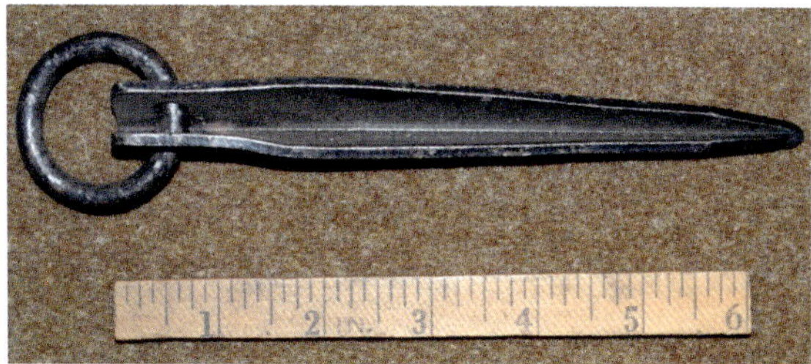

Type V ring piton manufactured by the Ames Corporation. The U.S. Army is credited with developing the ring piton.

U.S. Army ring piton, Preston, 1944.

Type II piton, Preston, 1944.

Mountain snap link.

Glacier Equipment

Early version of mountain crampons. Mountain crampons are large spikes fitted to climbing gear via straps. Mountain crampons came in two sizes: large and small. The spikes were 1½ in. long and engaged the ice on a glacier, providing secure footing and allowing soldiers to advance quickly. The crampons were also used for steep, slippery slopes such as grass slopes. (Harris)

Later-style crampons.

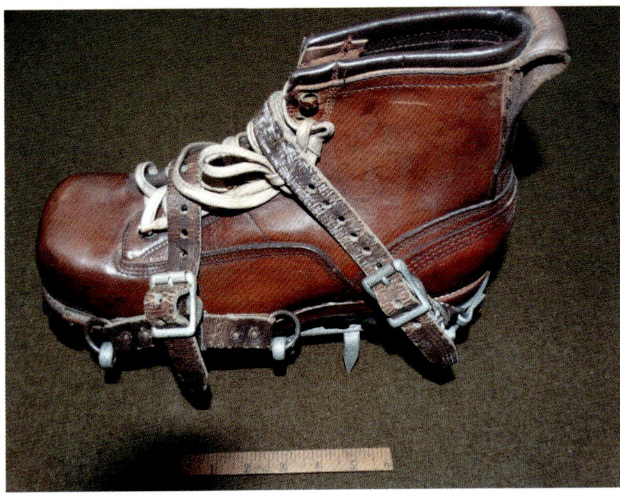

Crampons secured to ski/climbing boots.

Crampon Usage

Crampons are devices attached to mountain boots that increase traction on steep or icy slopes. With the 90 lb. rucksack and rifle, the mountain soldier must have the best possible traction when traversing icy terrain. When footwork on the mountain was less secure, soldiers put on crampons and strapped them to the mountain boots. During use, crampon straps tended to loosen and during breaks, it was standard procedure to tighten the straps.

There are three techniques for using crampons: flat-foot, front-of-foot, and hybrid. The flat-foot technique is used on moderate slopes where the foot is placed so that the sole is flat against the slope with as many spikes as possible engaged in the slope. The front-of-foot technique is used when the slope becomes steep, such as 45° or more. The soldier kicks the front of the mountain boot into the slope to securely engage the front spikes in the snow. This can become quite tiresome for the mountaineer, so a third hybrid method combined the two. In the hybrid method, one foot uses the front-of-foot method while the other is placed at about 90° from the foot and engaged in the flat-foot position in a duck-foot stance. The soldier rests occasionally on the foot that is turned out. During use, snow may accumulate under the crampon, limiting the bite into the mountain. The soldier may move the crampons from side to side against the snow surface to clear the snow. The ice axe can also help by banging it against the crampon to shake off the excess snow. When descending, soldiers have flexed knees with a stance wider than shoulder width, with the toes facing in the direction of travel to maintain balance.

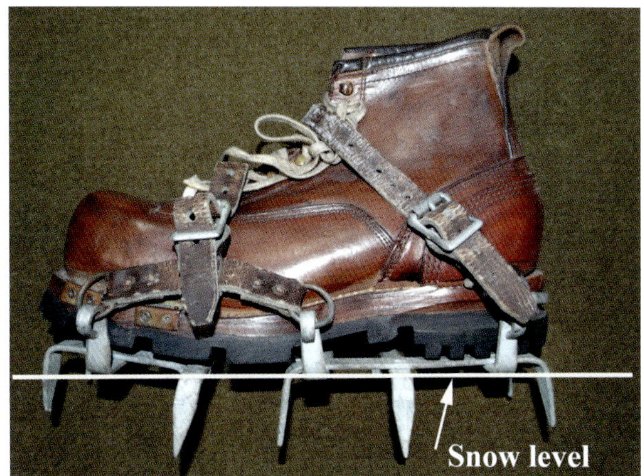

Flat-foot technique.

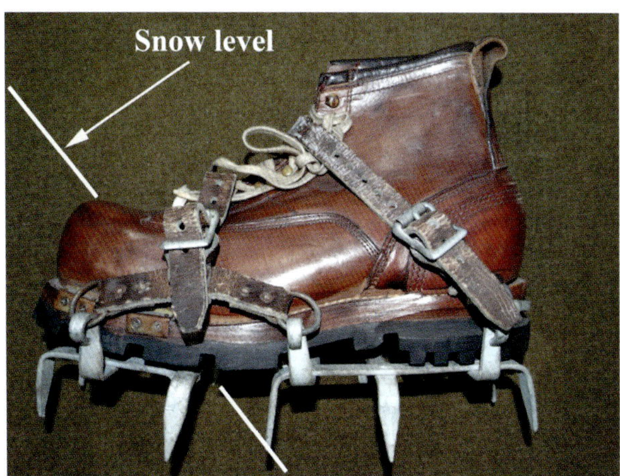

Front-of-foot technique.

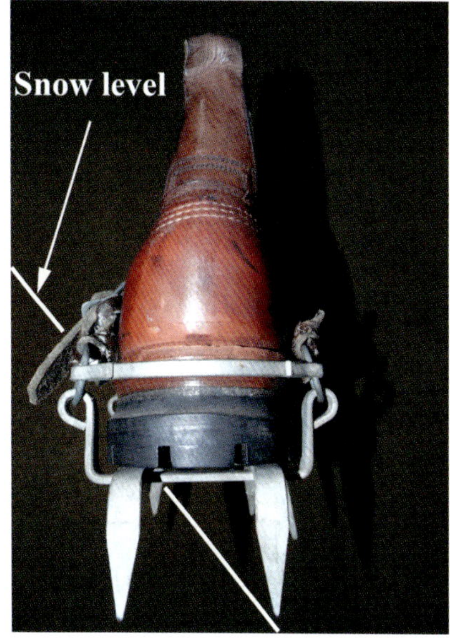

Hybrid technique. One foot is in the front-of-foot position, while the other is nearly perpendicular in a duck stance.

One way for a soldier to descend or ascend a steep slope was with the help of an ice axe. Crampon spikes are perpendicular to the slope.

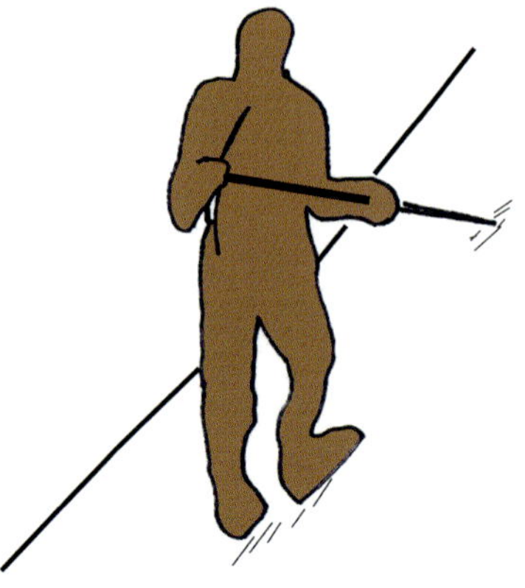

A soldier traversing an icy slope shows spikes perpendicular to the slope.

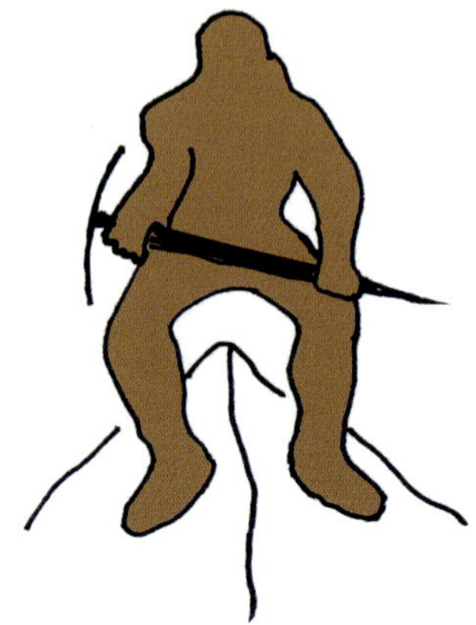

A soldier traversing an ice ridge.

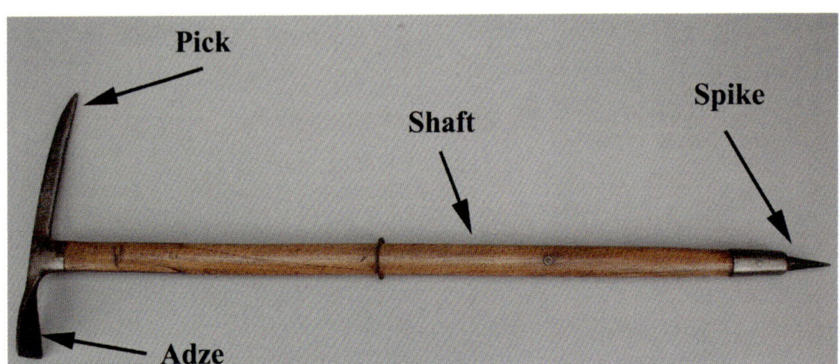

The ice axe is an essential tool for mountaineering. It aids in balance on irregular icy slopes when climbing, and if a soldier fell, he could use the axe to stop himself by digging in the axe—a self-arrest position. The use of an ice axe increases if the slope becomes steeper, surface conditions change, fatigue is setting in, or the consequence of a fall is severe, such as sliding down a slope and over a cliff. The mountain ice axe was adopted in 1942 by the Army for the 10th Mountain Division, who, at that time, were training at Camp Hale, Colorado. 36½ in. long with a 12½ in. head, this axe has a missing wrist strap, but the critical metal strap retaining ring remains. This ice axe is marked "US / AMES" on the pick. The pick was used to grip the ice and aid in self-arrest. The adze was a broad-base hoe to cut steps in the snow or ice, the shaft acting as a supporting cane for walking. The spike penetrated the snow and aided in ascending or descending a slope. (John Adams-Graf)

Close-up of stamping on a mountain axe manufactured by Ames. (John Adams-Graf)

Cooking Gear

Camping stove disassembled.

Fuel can. (Harris)

A typical camping stove layout along with the standard canteen cup, serving plate, mess kit, and utensils.

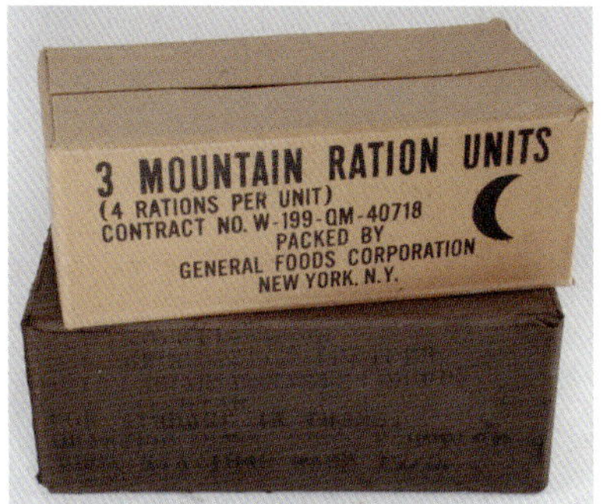

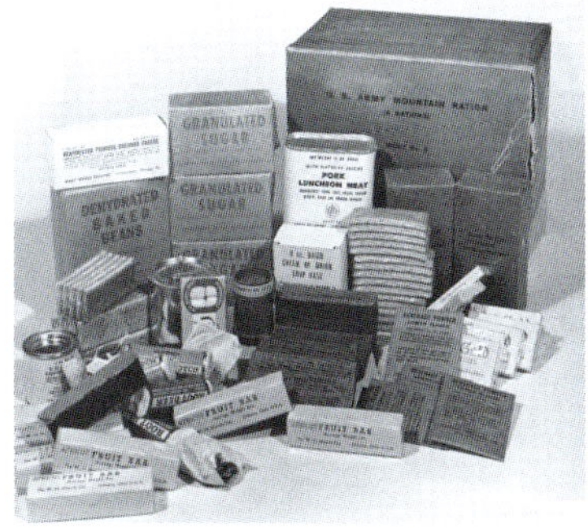

Special ration units for mountain troops. (John Adams-Graf)

First-pattern cook stove in self-contained aluminum cooking container dated 1944. The height of the stored unit is 8½ in. These were made to be self-contained and easily stored in the mountain pack. (John Adams-Graf)

COOKSET, MOUNTAIN

To remove cover, bring handles together and lift.
To close, place cover on pots with handles extending outward. Press down on cover, turning handles back into place, locking cover on pots.
FOR GOOD HEALTH, KEEP POTS CLEAN

Mountain cookset with the label instructing to "keep pots clean." In a typical infantry unit, garbage cans of boiling water were available to dip cooksets and thoroughly clean off adhered food. It was difficult to thoroughly clean cooksets without boiling water. Adhered food on cooksets could result in dysentery after the next meal. (John Adams-Graf)

The standard mess kit included a knife, fork, spoon, and two pans. The soldier could place the utensils and the divided serving pan on the long handle of the large pan and dip the whole kit in boiling water for cleaning.

Self-contained cookset consisting of two kettles (the smallest of the set is missing) and the lid with handles that unfold to make a frying pan. Designed for arctic conditions, these were issued to the 10th Mountain Division while training at Camp Hale. The paper label on top of the lid would probably be burned off during use. Outer kettle dated "U.S. / R.S.E. / 1944." (John Adams-Graf)

The standard-issue meat can pouch for the M1928 haversack, back and front. This belonged to Private Charles H. Meidner, Co. B, 602nd Field Artillery Battalion. The 602nd was a pack-mule unit. Meidner transferred from the Wisconsin National Guard. He was involved in several theaters of operation, including Italy, Kiska, France, and Germany. (John Adams-Graf)

Other Equipment

Taking a snow bath in camp.

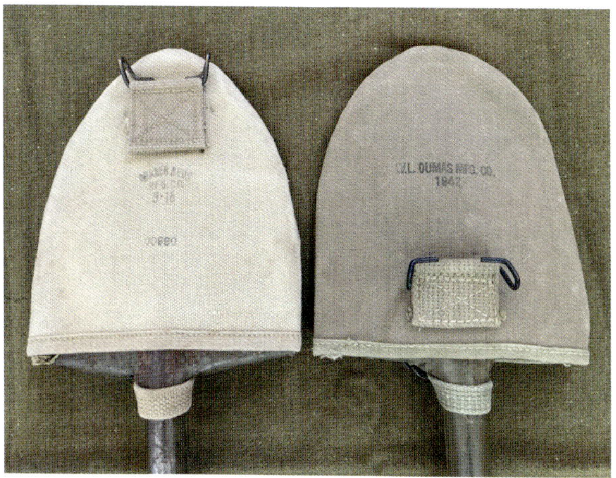

1910 T-handle shovel with mountain rucksack cover on the right with the hang tab at the bottom of the cover so it rides higher on the pack. This differed from the standard cover (left) with the hang tab at the top of the cover. (Harris)

Brush for clearing snow from uniforms, tents, and other items. This was considered a useless item by most 10th Mountain Division soldiers. They typically used these brushes as kindling to start campfires.

Packboard

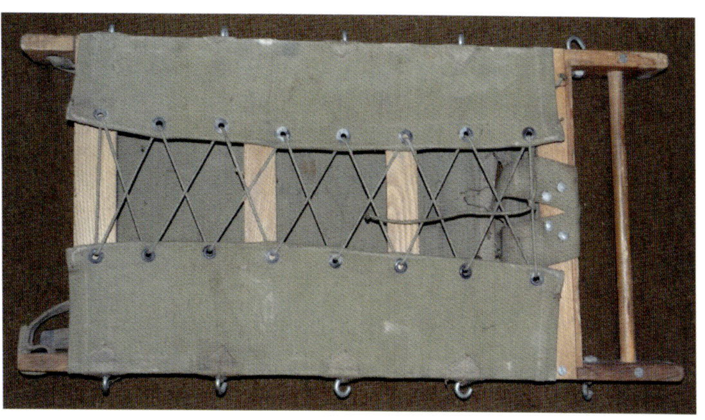

Outward side or cargo side of a 1943-vintage packboard. It had a wood frame and canvas cover for carrying cargo.

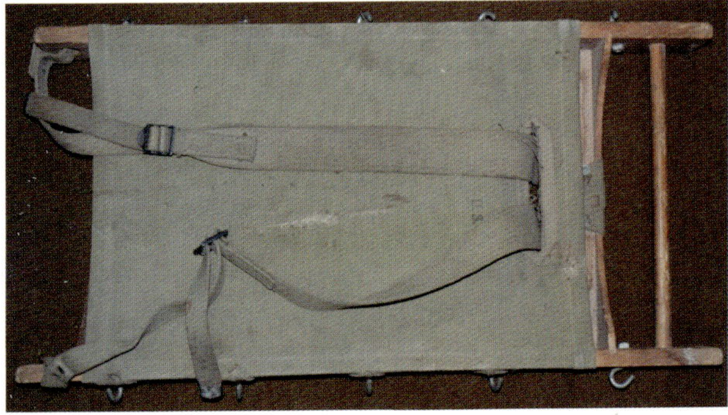

Soldier's side of the 1943-vintage packboard showing shoulder straps that were attached to the wood frame.

Huttig Sash & Door Co. is the manufacturer of this packboard.

This Signal Corps photo is captioned: "Past some strewn about German equipment, and a dead German soldier that someone thoughtfully covered up, go three men carrying howitzer ammunition to the top of the mountain, Mt. Belvedere area, Italy, 21 February 1945." The soldiers are using the 1944 packboard. (Signal Corps)

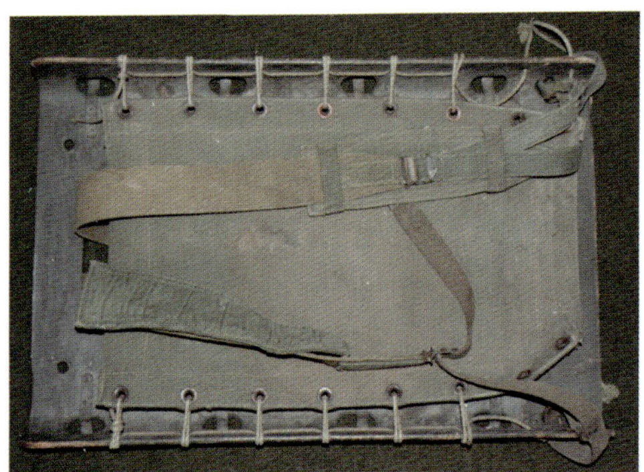

Inward (soldier's) side of a 1944-vintage packboard for carrying heavy items such as ammunition and other supplies.

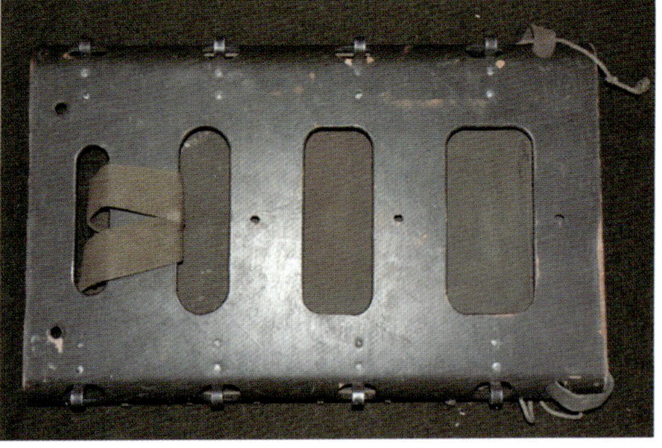

Outward side of a 1944 packboard for carrying heavy items such as ammunition and other supplies.

Rucksack

The M1928 haversack was inadequate for the mountain troops since it lacked the capacity for all the ski trooper equipment, and it had a center of mass high on the back, making it difficult to control while skiing. A pack with a lower center of mass was preferred while skiing. The first rucksack was adopted in 1941. It proved unsuccessful and was withdrawn from service and replaced with rucksacks manufactured under Tentative Specification J.Q.D. 88 Rucksack. This newer design had shoulder straps that held the frame more tightly to the soldier's back. Two straps were provided for the back flap, keeping the cover closed and pushing the load in the pockets more toward the back of the ski trooper. Four equipment bags were provided: two on each side for additional equipment. A new steel tubular frame was provided with bends conforming to the ski trooper's hips. The frame was also designed to join two skis to form a sled using ski adaptors.

Refinement of the rucksack design resulted in the Tentative Specification J.Q.D. 88B, which added webbing shoulder straps (eliminating the felt straps) and provided a means of easily attaching an M1 rifle to the pack. This rucksack was the primary design used by the 10th Mountain Division at Camp Hale. In August 1943, Quartermaster Tentative Specification J.Q.D. 88F was implemented, which changed the color of the rucksack to OD Shade 7, along with leather straps and roller buckles to ease securing the pockets in freezing conditions. Since the J.Q.D. 88B was already distributed to the 10th Mountain Division, very few J.Q.D. 88Fs would have been used by the 10th. Manufacturers of the rucksacks were American Fabrics, Atlantic Products, Avery Manufacturing, Baker-Lockwood Manufacturing, Hinson Manufacturing, Lichtenberger-Ferguson, Lyon & Coulson, Meese, Marrow & Douglass, Powers, Protections Products, Simmons, Varied Manufacturing, and Werner Siegmund. In 1943, the Quartermaster developed the 1943 "Jungle Pack," which all the military forces used. The 10th received these packs for testing and used them overseas.

A 1941-pattern J.Q.D. 88B canvas rucksack mounted on a steel-wire frame with three pockets outside the bag for extra gear. Brass snap hooks closed the two side pockets and the cover flap. It was made to U.S. Army Specification File No. 2971, July 7, 1941, by the Powers Company in 1942. The exterior flap is marked with "U.S." (John Adams-Graf)

A white cotton camouflage cover made by Lyon & Coulson and dated 1943. (John Adams-Graf)

Complete third-pattern mountain rucksack made according to Quartermaster Tentative Specification J.Q.D. 88B, dated August 26, 1942. This spec added a rifle-securing strap, a wire rifle snap hook on the right horn of rucksack frame, and a small hook on the left shoulder strap. It was the primary style of rucksack used by the 10th Mountain. It was made by Hinson Mfg. and dated 1942. (John Adams-Graf)

Third-pattern mountain rucksack showing both the belly strap and rifle strap. It was fitted with shoulder pads that were not included with the previous pattern. (John Adams-Graf)

A typical rule of thumb was to load the rucksack with items needed for a few days and to weigh between 33% and 50% of the soldier's weight. Food, ammunition, underwear, socks, and radio equipment would be a priority in the rucksack.

Complete, fourth-pattern mountain rucksack made according to Quartermaster Tentative Specification J.Q.D. 88F, dated August 1943, which changed the canvas color to OD 7 and replaced the roller buckles with double-bar buckles. This was the last style of rucksack issued to the 10th Mountain Division before they left Colorado. It was made by Protection Products Co. and is dated 1943. (John Adams-Graf)

The belly strap of the fourth-pattern mountain rucksack. (John Adams-Graf)

In 1943, as part of the Model 1943 uniform program, the U.S. Army developed a new set of accouterments to replace the M1928 Haversack. Commonly referred to as a "Jungle Pack," these packs were issued to a limited number of units for testing. The 10th Mountain Division left the United States with these new packs instead of their mountain rucksacks. Photo documentation reveals that these OD packs were worn by Marines in the Pacific Theater as well. This is a dark-olive pack, dated 1943, with a drawstring top, straps for contracting or expanding the pack size, and an open flap with a zippered pouch. The pack is fitted with the correct folding shovel carrier, shovel, and an undated OD 7 rifleman's belt with a 1942-dated first aid pouch. (John Adams-Graf)

Typical first aid pouch. (John Adams-Graf)

Troops of G Company, 2nd Battalion, 10th Mountain Division march down the street in newly liberated Verona, Italy, on April 26, 1945. Note the 1943 jungle packs used by the 10th instead of the mountain rucksacks. The theory behind the mountain rucksack was that it had a lower center of mass, which helped skiers. The jungle packs have a higher center of mass, which makes it easier to adjust the load while walking. (John Adams-Graf)

Weapons Used by the 10th Mountain Division

The 10th Mountain Division was equipped with the standard weapons supplied to divisions of the U.S. Army at that time. These included small arms such as the 1911 .45 cal. pistol all the way up to the 105 mm howitzer. This chapter describes the weapons used by the 10th in World War II, plus those tested but not used, which include the T32 37 mm infantry gun, the 37 mm antitank gun M3, the M8 pack howitzer, the 57 mm antitank gun, the 105 mm howitzer, the BAR, the M1903 rifle, the M1 rifle, the carbine, the Thompson submachine gun, the M3 grease gun, the M1911 pistol, the M1919 Browning machine gun, the M2 .50 cal. machine gun, the M20 75 mm recoilless rifle, the M2 60 mm mortar, the M1 81 mm mortar, and the bazooka.

While the 87th Infantry Regiment was at Fort Lewis, Washington, before they came to Camp Hale, they trained with broomsticks until rifles became available. Soldiers with sidearms got revolvers until the M1911 pistol was tested for reliability under cold conditions.

T32 37 mm field gun loaded on a mule. (U.S. Army)

T32 37 mm Field Gun

In late 1943, the U.S. Army began development of a light 37 mm gun, designated the T32, that could be handled by a rifle squad. The results from the Pacific Theater suggested that a lightweight 37 mm field gun would be helpful to forward units. The chamber of the T32 would accept the 5.69 in. M4 aircraft gun cartridge with a chamber pressure of 27,000 psi, firing an explosive projectile at 1,500 ft./sec. A canister antipersonnel round was available, essentially a large shotgun shell.

The gun used a tripod like the .50 cal. machine-gun tripod, modified to allow traverse and elevation of the gun. The tripod was not steady enough to absorb the weapon's recoil, and the gun had to be repositioned after each shot. The total weight was approximately 250 lb. Approximately 155 guns were sent to the Pacific in July 1944, but they were not readily accepted by the troops in the field. The T32 project was canceled, and the remaining guns were sent to the 10th Mountain Division in Italy in late 1944.

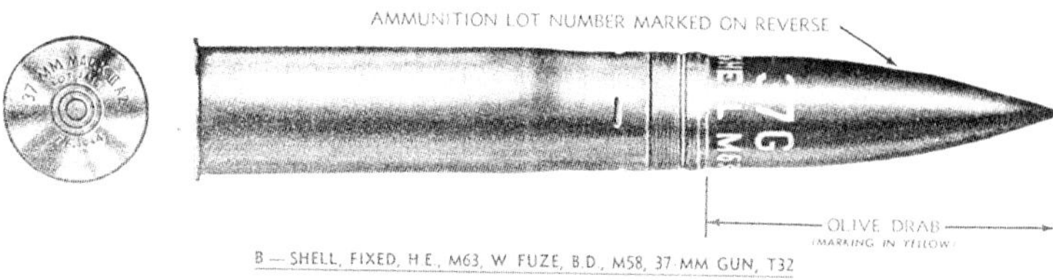

M63 H.E. cartridge used on the T32 field gun. (TM 9-246)

T32 37 mm field gun. (U.S. Army)

10th Mountain Division troops with T32 37 mm field guns on tripods. (U.S. Army)

M3 37 mm Gun

M3 37 mm gun carriage, the first field antitank gun used in World War II. (*U.S. 37 mm Gun in World War II*)

In 1936, the Germans became involved in the Spanish Civil War by providing aid to the Nationalists under Francisco Franco. The Germans also used this conflict to test their military equipment. The German 37 mm Pak 35/36 antitank gun was effective against enemy tanks. This did not go unnoticed by the U.S. Army, who procured two German 37 mm guns for development purposes. Larger-caliber guns were not considered because the U.S. Army wanted a light weapon to be handled by a squad-sized crew. Development continued, resulting in the M3 antitank gun. Watervliet Arsenal manufactured the gun, and Rock Island Arsenal produced the carriage. Initial models of the M3 had a gas deflector at the muzzle end, which was later removed as ineffective. The split-rail carriage had pneumatic tires, usually civilian truck tires. The 10th Mountain Division tested

M3 37 mm gun being towed by a Weasel at Camp Hale. (John Adams-Graf)

M3 37 mm gun on skis. (John Adams-Graf)

some M3 antitank guns at Camp Hale. Some were pulled into position with a Weasel using the conventional tires, while others had the tires removed and replaced with skis. Since field artillery battalions were attached to the 10th Mountain Division using the 75 mm pack howitzer, it was considered that the M3 37 mm gun did not have the punch of the 75 or 105 mm howitzer. The Pack 75 could be used as a direct-fire weapon or as a howitzer indirect-fire weapon, while the M3 was primarily a direct-fire weapon. Consequently, the M3 was not adopted by the 10th.

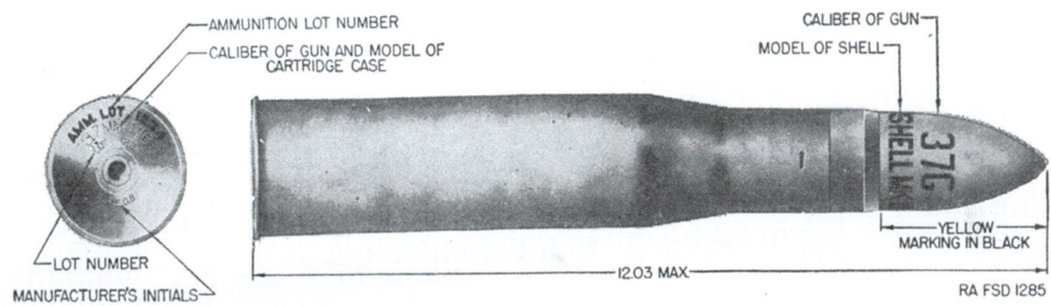

37 mm MK II cartridge used in the M3 37 mm gun. (*U.S. 37 mm Gun in World War II*)

M1A1 75 mm Pack Howitzer on Carriage M8

The M1A1 75 mm pack howitzer on M8 carriage could be broken down into eight major parts and carried by mules. This was often called the mountain gun.

The M1A1 pack howitzer, often called the mountain gun, was easily transported by pack animals in rugged terrain. The gun could be broken down into several pieces: rear rail and axle, front trail, top sleigh and cradle, bottom sleigh and recoil mechanism, breech, wheels, and gun tube. It could be used as a direct-fire or indirect-fire weapon. The field artillery battalions attached to the 10th Mountain Division used the M1A1 pack howitzer in training at Camp Hale and later in Italy along with the 105 mm howitzer. It could be hauled up the mountain, set up easily, and was able to fire on remote enemy positions with as few as four soldiers, although the standard crew was six. This was the second-most widely produced American howitzer in World War II. It was developed in the 1920s and standardized in 1927 as the M1 pack howitzer on carriage M1, as a field piece that could be moved over rugged terrain. Not many were produced in the 1930s, but in September 1940, the howitzer entered mass production until December 1944. Early production models had wooden wheels, which were later replaced with steel rims and civilian pneumatic truck tires.

M1A1 pack howitzer on skis for easy towing and to keep from sinking deep into snow. (John Adams-Graf)

75 mm Pack Howitzer M1A1 (TM 9-319)	
Weight of howitzer (with breech mechanism)	341 lb.
Weight of tube	221 lb.
Weight of tipping parts	839 lb.
Length of howitzer (with breech ring)	59 in.
Length of tube	(15.93 cal.) 47 in.
Rifling, number of grooves	28
Twist	Uniform, right-hand, one turn in 20 calibers
Diameter of bore	(2.95 in.) 75 mm
Type of breechblock	Horizontal sliding wedge
Weight of breech mechanism	121 lb.
Type of firing mechanism	Continuous pull
Muzzle velocity	
Shell, H.E., M48, with charge 4 (max.)	1,250 ft./sec.
Shell, H.E., M48, with charge 1 (min.)	700 ft./sec.
Range (max.) (Shell, H.E., M48 at 772.5 mils* elevation)	9,620 yd.
Rate of fire (equivalent full charge rounds in cool tube)	
First 30 seconds	16 rpm
First 4 minutes	6 rpm
First 10 minutes	5 rpm
Prolonged fire	150 rph
Maximum number of rounds which should be fired consecutively before cooling	60 rounds
Estimated accuracy life of tube (equivalent full charge rounds)	20,000 rounds
Data Pertaining to 75 mm howitzer carriage M8	
Time to emplace (paracrate loads)	7 min.
Time to emplace (pack loads)	3 min.
Weights	
Howitzer and carriage (complete with accessories)	1,440 lb.
Wheel with tire (each)	90 lb.
At lunette	40 lb.
Dimensions in traveling position, overall	
Length	126 in.
Width	50 in.
Height	33 in.
Road clearance	10 in.

Methods of transportation
Towed by prime mover (truck, ¼-ton, 4 × 4 or carrier, cargo, M29 or M29C)
Carried as a unit in airplanes C-46, C-47, or C-82
Carried as a unit in gliders CG-4A or CG-15A
Packed in paracrate loads for parachute delivery from airplanes C-46, C-47, C-82
In pack loads for animal transport

* 1 mil = 1/1,000 inch.

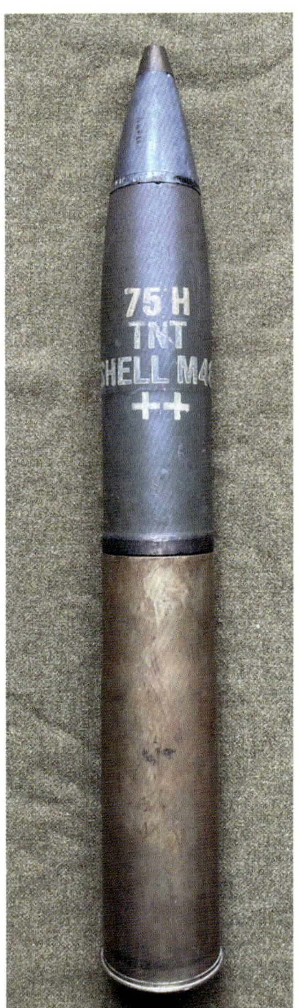

Cartridge 75 mm H.E. M41A1 and PD fuze M48A2. (Wszolek)

Cartridge 75 mm H.E.A.T. M66. (Wszolek)

75 mm salute cartridge case M18.

Cartridge case fired by the 604th Field Artillery at Camp Hale, 1943.

M1A2 57 mm antitank gun on M2 carriage.

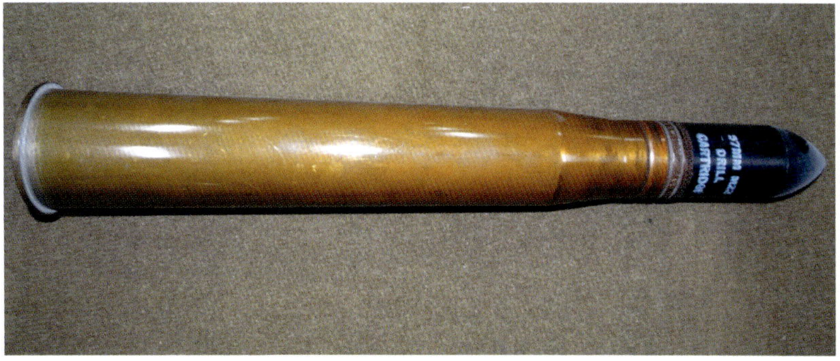

57 mm M22 drill cartridge.

M1A2 57 mm Antitank Gun

It became apparent in North Africa that the M3 37 mm antitank gun was inadequate in defeating the continual upgrades of German armor. This spurred the adoption of the 57 mm M1 antitank gun of British design. The Ordnance Board introduced the gun over the objection of the airborne units and the cavalry, who rejected it because it was too heavy. By 1943, the typical infantry division had the 57 mm gun. The WC-62 and WC-63 6 × 6 trucks were used to haul the M1 gun, which weighed 2,679 lb. The M1 gun was too heavy for the standard WC 51/52-series trucks that hauled the M3 37 mm gun. By mid-1944, the M1 57 mm gun was the standard antitank gun for the U.S. infantry in the European Theater. A gun crew for the 57 mm gun comprised six soldiers. It was a direct-fire weapon and did not work well in mountainous terrain. However, the gun was designed for action against tanks, which usually did not travel in mountainous terrain.

Gun, 57 mm M1A2 (TM 9-303)	
Weight of gun	755 lb.
Weight of tube and breech ring	505 lb.
Weight of tipping parts	1,142 lb.
Length of gun (muzzle to rear face of breech ring)	116.95 in.
Length of tube	112.20 in.
Length of bore (muzzle to front face of breech)	48.2 cal.
Length of bore (muzzle to front face of breech)	108.20 in.
Length of rifling	94.18 in.
Muzzle velocity (average velocity with a new gun)	
Cartridge, APC-T, M86	2,700 ft./sec.
Cartridge, AP-T, M70 (current productions)	2,950 ft./sec.
Range (maximum)	
Cartridge, APC-T, M86 at 266.7 mils or 15°	9,840 yd.
Cartridge, AP-T, M70 at 62.1 mils or 3.49°	3,500 yd.
Rate of fire, normal	15 rpm
Breechblock	Vertical sliding wedge
Carriages	
Weights and measurements are approximately the same for the 57 mm gun carriages M1, M1A1, M1A2, M1A3, and M2	
Time to emplace (normal)	1½ min.
Total weight without gun	1,945 lb.
Dimensions, traveling, position, overall	
Length (Carriages M1, M1A1, and M1A2)	15½ ft.
(Carriages M1A3 and M2)	16⅔ ft.
Width	75 in.
Height	50 in.
Road clearance	10 in.
Turning radius	9 ft. (approx.)
Limits of elevation	
Maximum (degrees or mils)	15° or 266.7 mils
Depression (degrees or mils)	–5° or –88.9 mils
Elevation per turn of hand wheel	10.7 mils

Limits of traverse (right or left)	45°
Diameter of circle of emplacement	12 ft. (approx.)
Traverse per turn of hand wheel (Carriages M1 and M1A1)	5.4 mils
Recoil mechanism	
Model	M12
Maximum allowable recoil	31½ in.
Elevation at which maximum recoil occurs (degrees or mils)	15° or 266.7 mils
Type of recoil mechanism	Hydrospring
Type of counter-recoil mechanism	Spring
Weight of hydrospring	99 lb.
Weight of Slipper (sleigh)	95 lb.
Tires	
Type and size	8.00 × 16 combat
Pressure	30 psi
Brakes, type	Hand parking

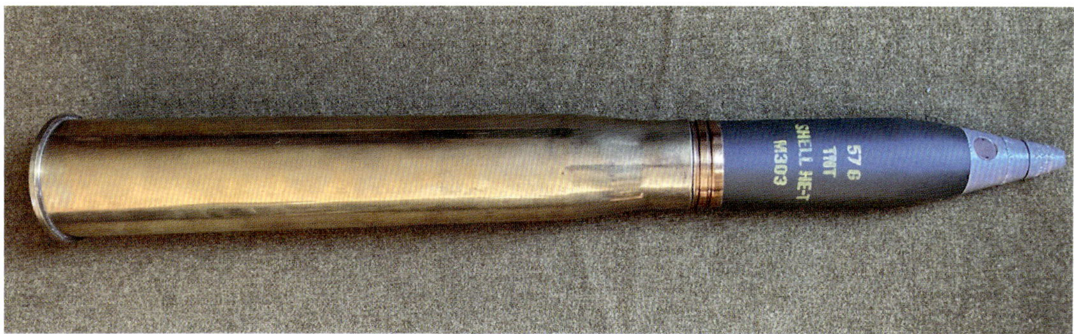

Cartridge, armor-piercing, M303 for the M1 57 mm gun and the British 6-pounder. (Wszolek)

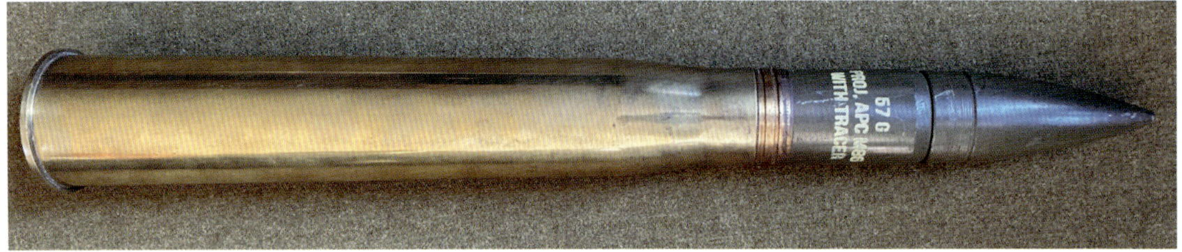

Cartridge, armor-piercing, APC M86 for the M1 57 mm gun and the British-6 pounder; muzzle velocity 2,700 ft./sec., explosive projectile. (Wszolek)

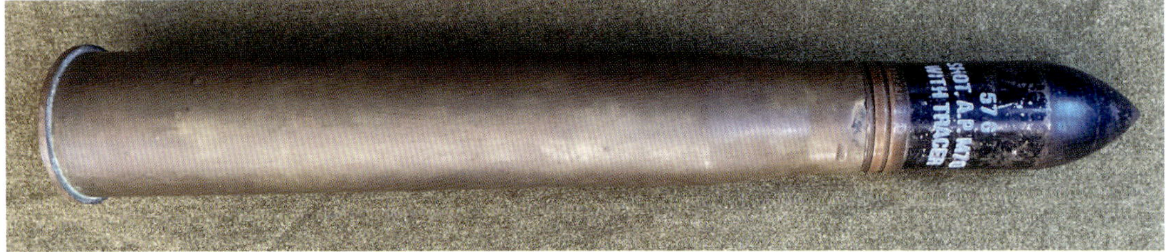

Cartridge, armor-piercing, AP-T M70 for the M1 57 mm gun and the British 6-pounder; muzzle velocity 2,950 ft./sec., solid projectile with tracer. (Wszolek)

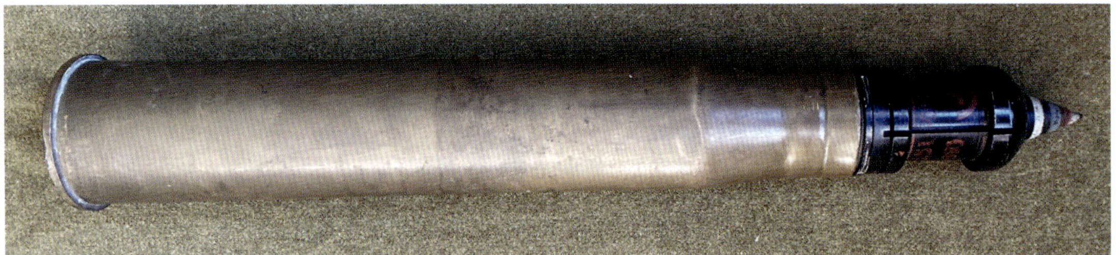

6-pounder (57 mm) armor-piercing discarding sabot, which entered service in the first half of 1944. The British produced and provided it in limited quantities to American units equipped with the M1 57 mm antitank gun. Sabot came out at about 4,000 ft./sec., so it could penetrate much thicker armor. (Wszolek)

105 mm Howitzer

After World War I, the U.S. Army Ordnance Department became interested in developing a light field howitzer. After a captured German 105 mm howitzer was inspected, the U.S. M1920 105 mm howitzer was developed. In December 1927, the 105 mm howitzer became standard with nomenclature M1 or carriage M1. Due to budget cuts in the military, only 14 M1 howitzers had been manufactured by 1933. A redesign was introduced in 1940 with the M2A1 gun using modified ammunition and the M2 carriage, which could be towed by trucks rather than horses. The gun was heavy for its caliber, contributing to its field longevity. The 105 mm howitzer was the standard light howitzer used by the U.S. Army in World War II. Production started in 1941. The gun was found to be accurate and to deliver a strong punch. The high-explosive fixed ammunition made the howitzer adequate for supporting infantry units. Many countries adopted the howitzer after the war. Artillery units attached to the 10th Mountain Division used the 105 mm howitzer to augment the 75 mm pack howitzer.

Right rear view of the 105 mm howitzer. (TM 9-325)

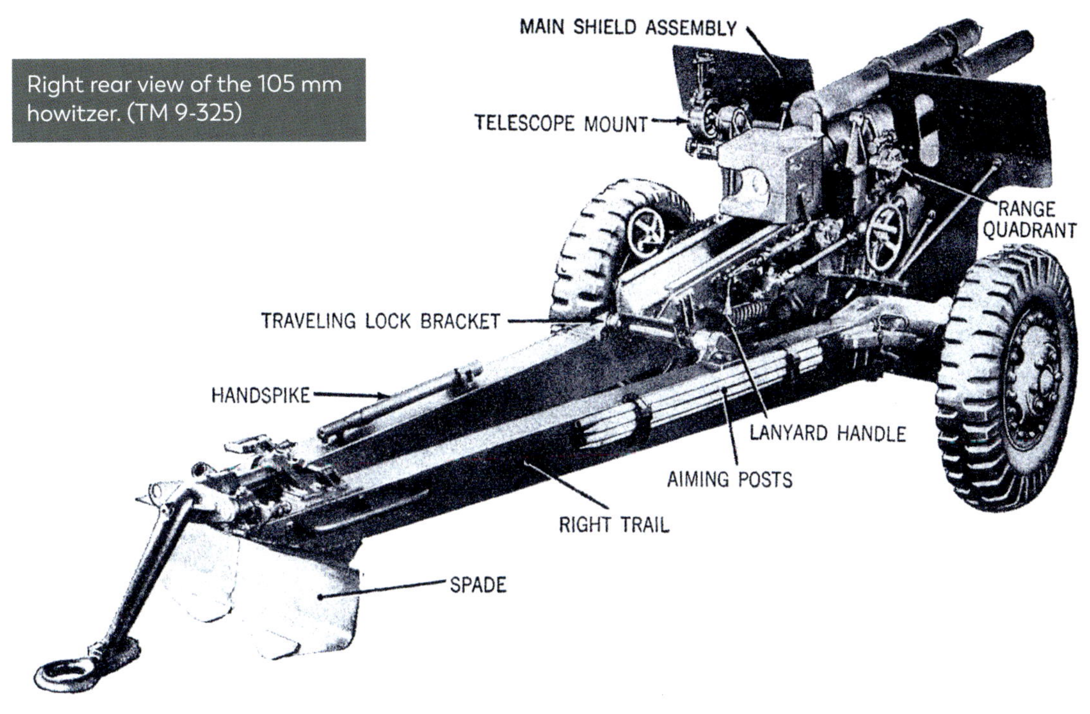

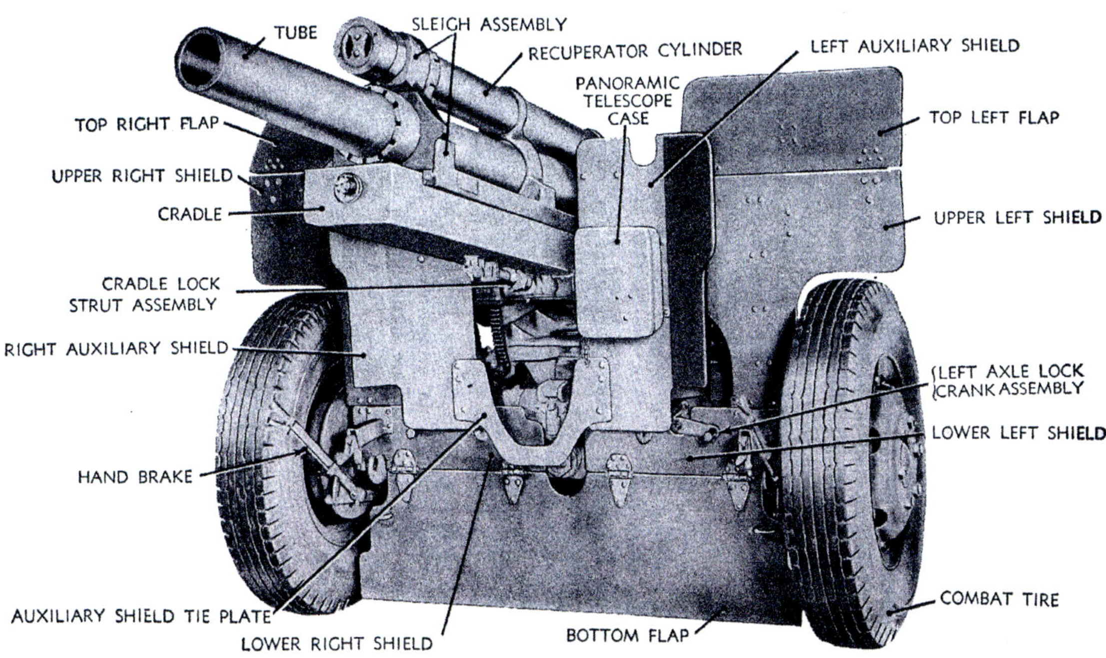

Left front view of the 105 mm howitzer. (TM 9-325)

105 mm howitzer.

105 mm howitzer on skis. The 10th Mountain Division rarely used this setup. (U.S. Army)

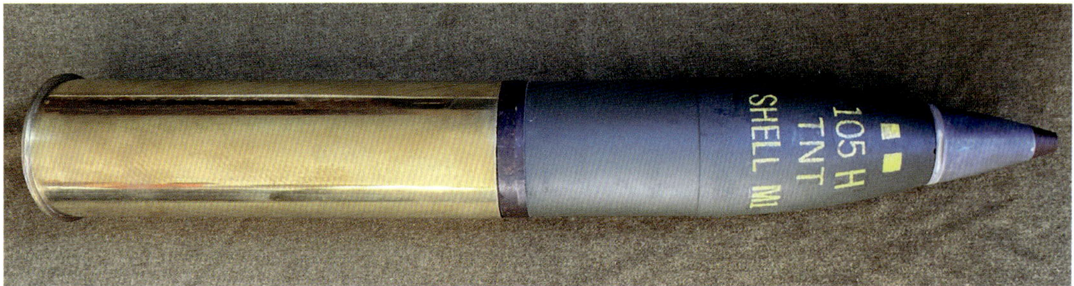

Cartridge semi-fixed M1 TNT for the 105 mm M2A1 howitzer. Semi-fixed ammunition allowed the projectile to be separated from the cartridge case so that the propellant charge could be adjusted. (Wszolek)

Cartridge semi-fixed M67 H.E.A.T. for the 105 mm M2A1 howitzer. (Wszolek)

Howitzer M2A1 (TM 9-1325)	
Caliber of howitzer	105 mm (4.134 in.)
Total weight of howitzer (tube and breech mechanism) (approx.)	1,064 lb.
Weight of tube (approx.)	706 lb.
Weight of tube and breech ring (approx.)	973 lb.
Weight of tipping parts (howitzer, recoil mechanism, cradle, sight mount, and range quadrant) (approx.)	2,028 lb.
Length of howitzer (muzzle to rear face of breech ring)	101.35 in.
Length of tube	93.05 in.
Length of bore	78.02 in.
Muzzle velocity (average velocity with a new howitzer)	
Shell, H.E. (maximum zone charge, carriage M2)	1,550 ft./sec.
Shell, H.E.A.T. (carriage M2)	1,250 ft./sec.
Range (maximum)	
Shell, H.E. (maximum zone charge at 778.6 mils, carriage M2)	12,205 yd.
Shell, H.E.A.T. (154.6 mils, carriage M2)	3,500 yd.
Shell, H.E.A.T. (778.1 mils, carriage M2)	8,590 yd.
Shell, H.E.A.T. (152.5 mils, motor carriage M7)	3,500 yd.
Rate of fire: Normal	2 rpm
Maximum	4 rpm
Type of breechblock	Horizontal sliding
Weight of breechblock (approx.)	74 lb.

Right-side-view sketch of a 105 mm howitzer.

Carriage, Howitzer, 105 mm (TM 9-1325)		
Time to emplace (normal)		3 min.
Weights: Howitzer and carriage	**M2A1**	**M2A2**
(complete with accessories, traveling position) (approx.)	4,475 lb.	4,980 lb.
Wheel with combat tire (9.00 × 20) (approx.)	287 lb.	287 lb.
Wheel with combat tire and hub (approx.)	345 lb.	345 lb.
At lunette (approx.)	235 lb.	235 lb.
Dimensions in traveling position, overall		
Length (approx.)	19⅔ ft.	19⅔ ft.
Width (over hub caps) (approx.)	84½ in.	84½ in.
Height (approx.)	60 in.	62 in.
Road clearance (approx.)	15½ in.	13 in.
Turning radius (approx.)	11 ft.	11 ft.
Towed by prime mover		
2½-ton	6 × 6 cargo truck	6 × 6 cargo truck
13-ton	High-speed tractor M5	High-speed tractor M5

Limits of elevation	M2A1	M2A2
Maximum (approx.)	1,180 mils	1,180 mils
Depression (approx.)	–84 mils	–84 mils
Elevation per turn of hand wheel	10 mils	10 mils
Limits of traverse (degrees right or left) (approx.)	23°	23°
Diameter of circle of emplacement (approx.)	21.1 ft.	21.1 ft.
Traverse per turn of hand wheel		
(screw-type traversing mechanism)	19 mils	19 mils
(worm and rack traversing mechanism)	21 mils	21 mils
Recoil mechanism		Model M2A1
Normal length of recoil		42 in.
Maximum allowable recoil		44 in.
Elevation at which maximum recoil occurs (maximum elevation)		1,180 mils
Type		Hydro-pneumatic
Weight (complete with sleigh and filled) (approx.)		463 lb.
Initial gas pressure at 70°F (21°C) without reserve oil		1,100 psi
Tires		
Type and size		9.00 × 20 combat
Pressure (combat or standard)		40 psi

On-carriage Sighting Equipment

Range Quadrant: M4

Telescope Mount M21AI with Panoramic Telescope: M12A2 or M5A3

Telescope Mount M23 with Elbow Telescope: M16

Browning M1918 .30 Cal. Automatic Rifle

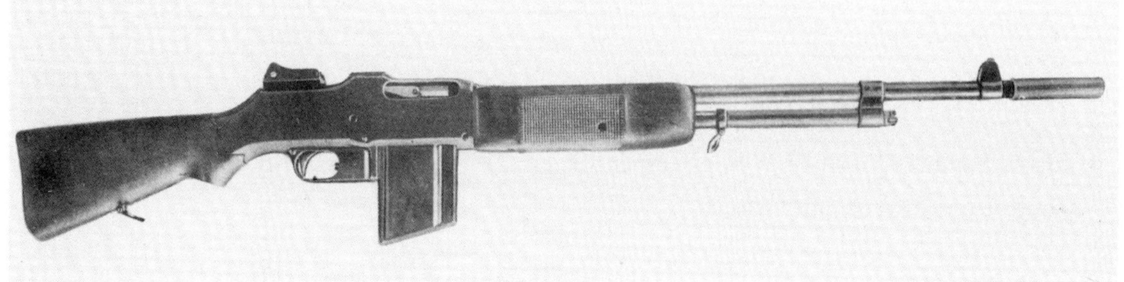

John Browning started with the BAR (Browning automatic rifle) design in 1910. He felt that an automatic weapon using the standard U.S. .30-06 cartridge would enhance the firepower of a squad. A demonstration of the weapon held in February 1917 showed its effectiveness, and the Colt Patent Firearms Company was awarded a contract for production. Colt was at capacity to produce weapons, so Winchester Repeating Arms Company took over as the main contractor to produce the weapon. The U.S. 79th Infantry Division was the first to receive BARs. They used the weapon in September 1918, and it proved very effective. During the Meuse-Argonne Offensive, the BARs proved impressive; France requested over 15,000 rifles. During the 1920s and 1930s, the BAR was deployed in smaller Regular Army units, with some issued to the National Guard. Some BARs were stolen from armories and used in criminal activities such as those of Bonnie and Clyde. The BAR was issued to Naval and Marine units. At the beginning of World War II, the Ordnance Department tried to make the BAR into a squad machine gun by adding a bipod, stock rest (monopod), and flash hider, resulting in the M1918A2. The weapon's accuracy improved, but the increase in weight made it more difficult to use in dynamic battlefield conditions. Consequently, many soldiers removed the bipod, monopod, and flash hider to save weight, making it easier to deploy. The BAR had a strong recoil spring, making it difficult to aim accurately because of the recoil rebound. It took time to change the barrel, and the limited magazine capacity of 20 rounds was less effective than other Allied machine guns. The BAR worked reasonably well in service conditions if the weapon was stripped and cleaned frequently.

10th Mountain Division troops practicing with a BAR. (U.S. Army)

Rifle, Automatic, Cal. .30, Browning, M1918 (TM 9-2200)	
Weight (with sling, magazine, and flash hider)	16½ lb.
Length (overall)	47.6 in.
Weight of moving parts	2¼ lb.
Weight of barrel	3.65 lb.
Length of barrel	24.07 in.
Length of rifling	21.41 in.; 71.1 cal.
Rifling: number of grooves	4
R.H. twist; 1 turn in	33.3 cal.; 10 in.
Depth of grooves	0.004 in.
Cross-sectional area of bore	0.0740 sq. in.
Type of mechanism	Gas operated
Feeding device	Magazine
Capacity of feeding device	20 rounds
Rate of fire on automatic (normally fired on semi-automatic)	500–600 rpm
Cooling	Air
Sight radius	31.1 in.
Trigger pull	10 lb. max; 6 lb. min
Normal pressure	50,000 psi
Ammunition types	Ball, AP, tracer

The Browning automatic rifle (BAR) was a formidable weapon in World War II. Although heavy, it put out fire at a high rate, making it effective against enemy troops. The Germans would often try to knock out the BAR carrier first to limit the firepower of an American unit.

World War I soldier demonstrating a Browning automatic rifle, 1918. (Wikimedia Commons)

Browning M1918A2 .30 Cal. Automatic Rifle

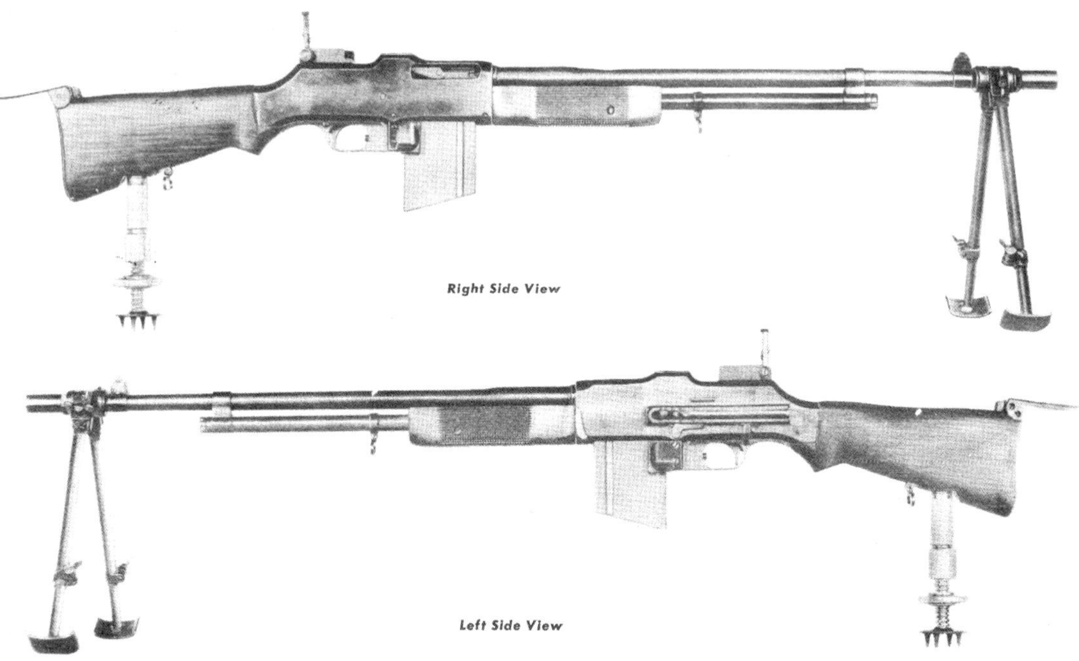

Rifle, Automatic, Cal. .30, Browning, M1918A2 (TM 9-2200)	
Weight complete	22 lb.
Weight bipod	2.69 lb.
Weight stock support	0.81 lb.
Weight without bipod and stock support	18½ lb.
Length	47.8 in.
Weight of moving parts	2¼ lb.
Weight of barrel	3.65 lb.
Length of barrel	24.07 in.
Length of rifling	21.41 in.; 71.1 cal.
Rifling: number of grooves	4
R.H. twist; 1 turn in	33.3 cal.; 10 in.
Depth of grooves	0.004 in.
Cross-sectional area of bore	0.0740 sq. in.
Type of mechanism	Gas operated

Feeding device	Magazine
Capacity of feeding device	20 rounds
Rate of fire	500–600 rpm (fast automatic)
	300–350 rpm (slow automatic)
Cooling	Air
Sight radius	31.1 in.
Trigger pull	10 lb. max; 6 lb. min.
Normal pressure	50,000 psi
Ammunition type	Ball, AP, tracer

M1903 .30 Cal. Rifle

Rifle, U.S., Cal. .30, M1903A1 (TM 9-2200)	
Weight (with bayonet M1905: 9.8 lb.)	8.8 lb.
Length (overall)	43.4 in.
Length of barrel	24 in.
Length of rifling	21.28 in., 70.7 cal.
Rifling: number of grooves	4
R.H. twist; 1 turn in	33.3 cal.; 10 in.
Depth of groves	0.004 in.
Cross-sectional area of bore	0.074 sq. in.
Type of mechanism	Manual (turn bolt)

Feeding device	Clip
Capacity of feeding device	5 rounds
Cooling	Air
Sight radius	21.1 in.
Trigger pull	6 lb. max; 4 lb. min.
Normal pressure	50,000 psi
Ammunition types	Ball, AP, tracer

The bolt-action rifle M1903 was copied from the German Mauser M1893 after the 1898 war with Spain, where Spanish forces equipped with the M1893 were able to hold off American forces equipped with older, less-efficient rifles. The M1903 was adopted as the standard infantry rifle in June 1903 and was first used in combat in the Philippine–American War. It was used during World War I but was replaced by the semi-automatic M1 Garand in 1936. The M1903 was still in use at the beginning of World War II since the M1 rifle was limited in availability. The M1903 with a scope was used as a sniper rifle in World War II. Snipers in the 10th Mountain Division used the M1903.

M1903 rifle with sniper scope. (U.S. Army)

M1 .30 Cal. Rifle, Garand

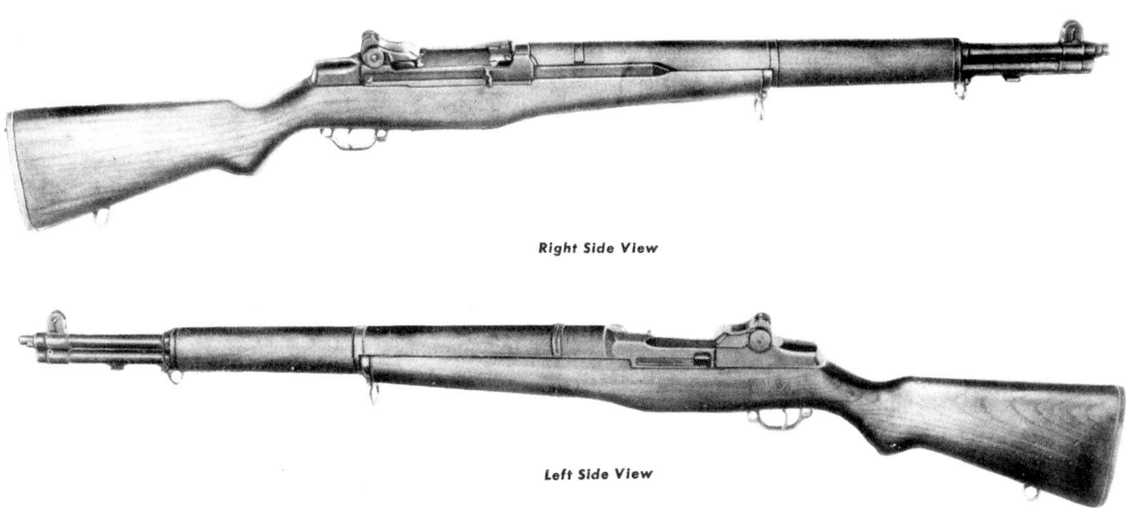
Right Side View

Left Side View

Rifle, Cal. .30 M1, Garand (TM 9-2200)	
Weight (with bayonet M1905: 10½ lb.)	9½ lb.
Length (overall)	43.6 in.
Length of barrel	24 in.
Length of rifling	21.30 in.; 70.8 cal.
Rifling: number of grooves	4
R.H. twist; 1 turn in	33.3 cal.; 10 in.
Depth of grooves	0.004 in.
Cross-sectional area of bore	0.074 sq. in.
Type of mechanism	Gas-operated semi-automatic
Feeding device	Clip
Capacity of feeding device	8 rounds
Rate of fire	Semi-automatic
Cooling	Air
Sight radius	27.9 in. at 100 yd. range
Trigger pull	7½ lb. max; 4½ lb. min.
Normal pressure	50,000 psi
Ammunition types	Ball, AP, tracer

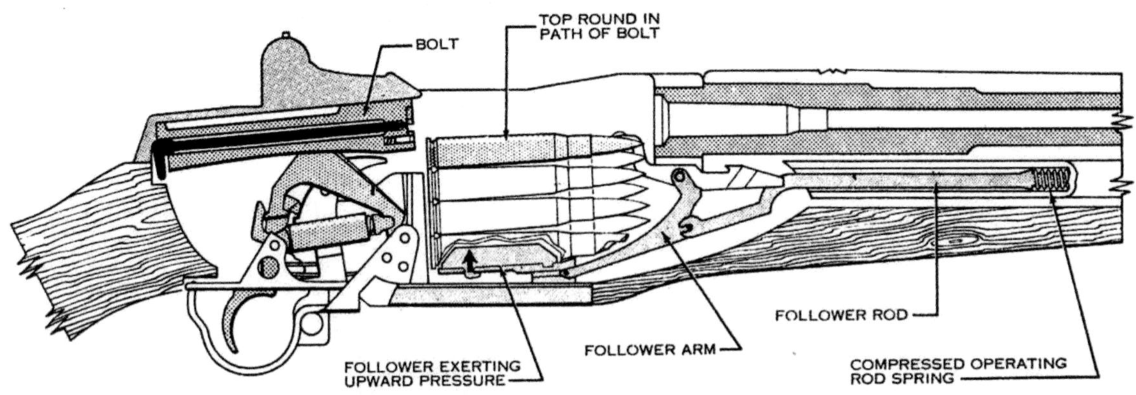

Drawing of the M1 showing the ammunition feed and semi-automatic firing mechanism. (FM 23-5)

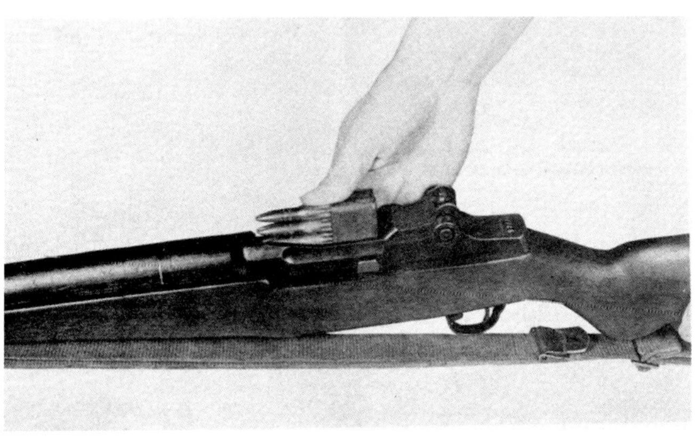

View showing how to load an M1 with the eight-round clip. As soon as the clip is loaded, the bolt immediately closes, loading the first round. If the person loading does not get the thumb out of the way, it can get caught, resulting in an injury called M1 thumb. (FM 23-5)

John Garand, who worked at the United States Army Springfield Armory, started working on a .30 cal. semi-automatic rifle and, in 1924, manufactured four prototypes of the M1922. Several tests were performed on other manufacturers' prototypes of semi-automatic rifles along with the Garand by the Cavalry Board. The Garand was dropped from the competition. In further testing in July 1929, the Garand was reinstated with some modifications. By 1932, the Army directed all resources to developing and improving the M1 Garand. On August 3, 1933, the semi-automatic rifle .30 cal. M1 was adopted, and 50 rifles were sent to infantry units and 25 to cavalry units. The M1 was standardized on January 9, 1936. The production of M1 rifles increased to 600 per day by January 10, 1941, and the U.S. Army was fully equipped with M1s by the end of 1941. This weapon was used by most troops in the 10th Mountain Division.

Rifle competition with the M1 at Camp Hale. (John Adams-Graf)

M1 .30 Cal. Carbine

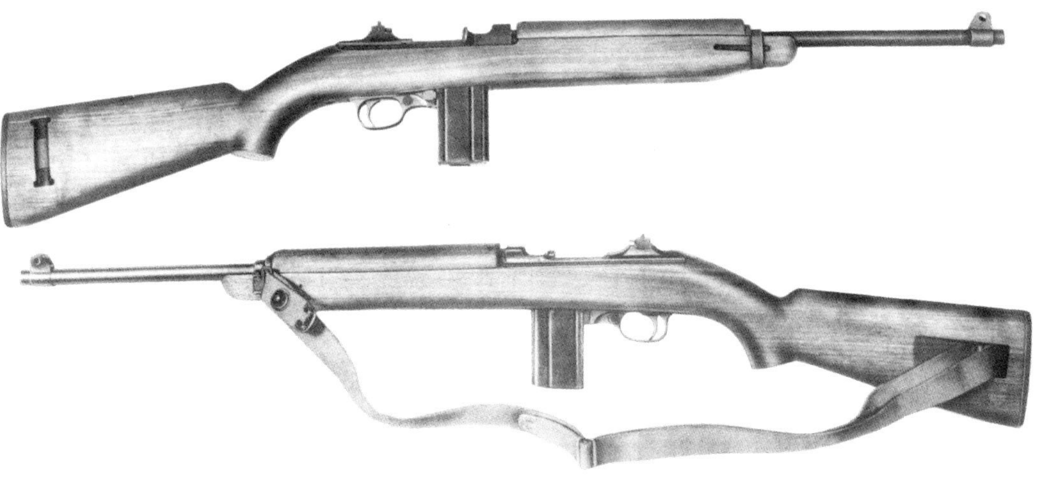

Carbine, Cal. .30, M1 (TM 9-2200)	
Weight	5.2 lb.
Length (overall)	35.6 in.
Length of barrel	18 in.
Length of rifling	16.77 in.; 55.7 cal.
Rifling: number of grooves	4
R.H twist; 1 turn in	66.6 cal.; 20 in.
Depth of grooves	0.0040 in.
Cross-sectional area of bore	0.074 sq. in.
Type of mechanism	Gas operated; semi-automatic
Feeding device	Magazine
Capacity of feeding device	15 rounds
Rate of fire	Semi-automatic
Cooling	Air
Sight radius	21.4 in.
Trigger pull	6 lb. max; 4 lb. min.
Normal pressure	38,000 psi
Ammunition types	Ball

In the late 1930s, the M1 Garand was considered too heavy for support troops such as artillery troops, staff officers, radio personnel, and other specialized noncombatants. Many soldiers found it needed to be slung diagonally across the back, preventing the use of their backpacks. The development of airborne units resulted in a request for a lighter rifle weighing about half as much as the M1. The U.S. Army decided that a carbine-type weapon (shorter version of a rifle) should be designed with a specification of a maximum weight of 5 lb., an effective range of 300 yd., and an optional folding stock for paratroopers. Winchester began to design a lightweight weapon. The company hired David Marshall Williams, who was still in the North Carolina minimum security prison, as a skilled weapons designer. His release was granted, and he was able to join Winchester, where he worked on a short-stroke, gas-piston design, among other firearm designs. Winchester engineers and Williams developed a prototype G30 rifle, which, after many iterations, resulted in the standardized M1 carbine on October 22, 1941.

The M1 carbine was not designed as a primary assault weapon. It was issued to officers, paratroopers, noncommissioned officers, other service-related front-line troops, and soldiers operating crew-served weapons. The troops liked the M1 carbine because of its light weight, small size, and firepower for such a small weapon.

10th Mountain Division soldiers with M1 carbines. (John Adams-Graf)

Thompson .45 Cal. Submachine Gun

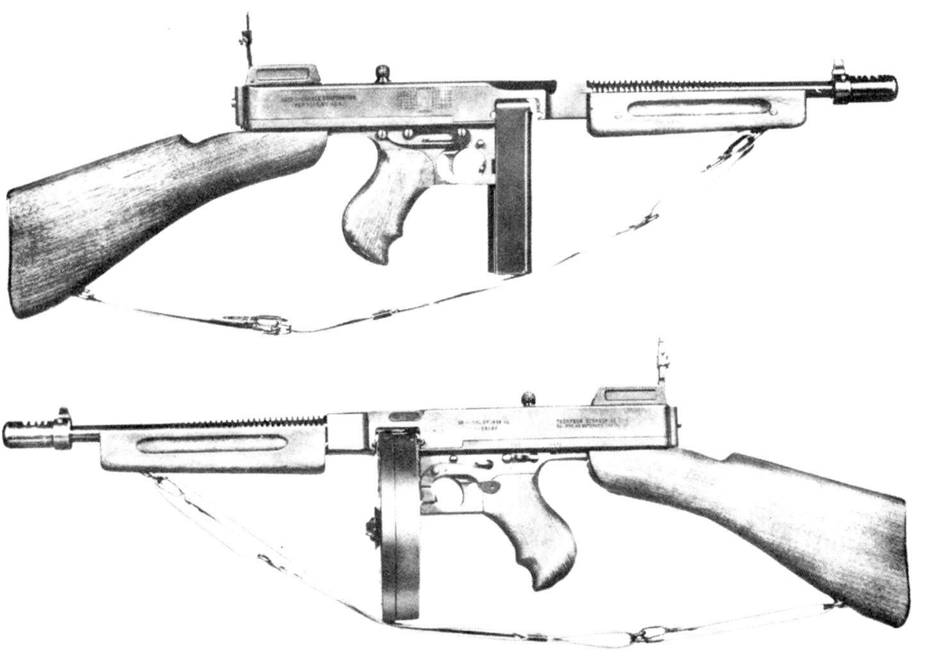

Gun, Submachine, Cal. .45, Thompson, M1928A1 (TM 9-2200)	
Weight (without magazine)	10.8 lb.
Length (overall) (with compensator)	33.7 in.
Weight of recoiling parts	1.62 lb.
Weight of barrel	¾ lb.
Length of barrel	10.52 in.
Length of rifling	10.12 in.; 22.8 cal.
Rifling: number of grooves	6
R.H. twist; 1 turn in	36 cal.; 16 in.
Depth of grooves	0.0035 in.
Cross-sectional area of bore	0.1581 sq. in.
Type of mechanism	Blowback
Feeding device	Magazine
Capacity of feeding device	20 or 50 rounds
Rate of fire	725 rpm

Cooling	Air
Sight radius	22.3 in.
Trigger pull	14 lb. max; 10 lb. min.
Normal pressure	17,000 psi
Ammunition types	Ball, tracer

Brigadier General John T. Thompson is credited with the invention of the Thompson submachine gun. There was considerable research and development of the machine gun before the end of World War I, but prototypes arrived too late to be used in the war. In 1919, the Auto-Ordnance board officially adopted the M1928A1 "Thompson" submachine gun to be used as a high-volume weapon in trench warfare. Production started in 1921 and was available to civilians but was expensive, resulting in poor sales. The machine gun gained notoriety because of gun battles between law enforcement and Prohibition-era gangsters. In 1926, a muzzle brake (Cutts compensator) was added to the weapon. In 1938, the Thompson submachine gun was adopted by the U.S. Army in two versions: the M1928A1 could accept both the drum and stick magazines, had a Cutts compensator, had cooling fins on the barrel, and a charging handle on top of the receiver. As requested by the U.S. military, the M1 and M1A1 simplified versions of the submachine gun used the stick magazine only, had a simplified rear sight, no cooling fins or compensator, and a charging handle on the side of the receiver. Over 1.5 million Thompsons were produced during World War II. They were used by scouts, non-commissioned officers, patrol leaders, commissioned officers, tank crews, and raiders.

M3 "Grease Gun"

M3 "grease gun." (Wikimedia Commons)

The U.S. Army adopted the M3 .45 cal. submachine gun in late 1942. It fired the same ammunition as the Thompson submachine gun but was much lighter and cheaper to mass produce. It was intended as a replacement for the higher-cost Thompson submachine gun. It was manufactured from stamped parts rather than more expensive machined parts but was less accurate than the Thompson. 10th Mountain troops used both versions.

10th Mountain Division soldier with a "grease gun," which was an economical replacement for the Thompson submachine gun. (John Adams-Graf)

M1911A1 .45 Cal. Semi-Automatic Pistol

M1911A1. (TM 9-2200)

Pistol, Automatic, Cal. .45, M1911A1 (TM 9-2200)	
Weight	2.44 lb.
Length (overall)	8.6 in.
Weight of recoiling parts	1.12 lb.
Weight of barrel	0.2 lb.
Length of barrel	5.03 in.
Length of rifling	4.08 in.; 9.2 cal.
Rifling: number of grooves	6
L.H. twist; 1 turn in	36 cal.; 16 in.
Depth of grooves	0.0039 in.
Cross-sectional area of bore	0.1581 sq. in.
Type of mechanism	Short recoil
Feeding device	Magazine
Capacity of feeding device	7 rounds
Cooling	Air
Sight radius	6½ in.
Trigger pull	6½ lb. max; 5½ lb. min.
Normal pressure	17,000 psi
Ammunition types	Ball

John Browning designed the Colt M1911 semi-automatic pistol, which became the standard sidearm for the U.S. Army in 1911. Approximately 2.7 million were produced during its service life. Officers, non-commissioned officers, tank crews, and others not carrying rifles used this sidearm.

10th Mountain Division soldier carrying an M1911 semi-automatic pistol. (John Adams-Graf)

M1919A4 Browning .30 Cal. Machine Gun

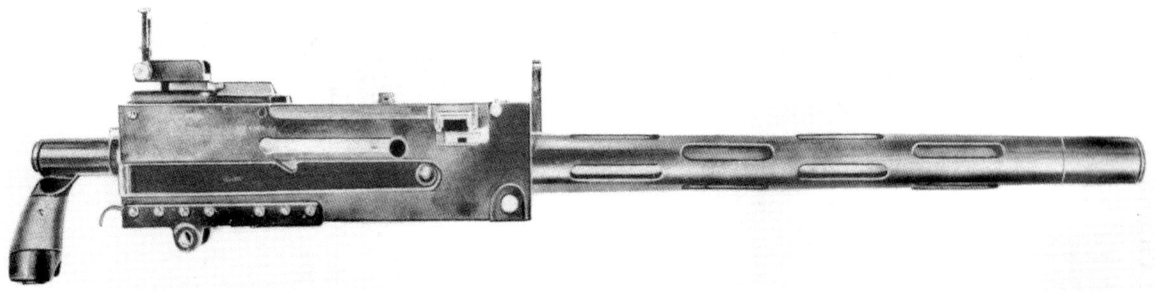

Gun, Machine, Cal. .30, Browning, M1919A4, Flexible (TM 9-2200)	
Weight	31 lb.
Length (overall)	41.11 in.
Weight of recoiling parts	11.7 lb.
Weight of barrel	7.35 lb.
Length of barrel	24 in.
Length of rifling	21.38 in.; 71 cal.
Rifling: number of groves	4
R.H. twist; 1 turn in	33.3 cal.; 10 in.
Depth of grooves	0.004 in.
Cross-sectional area of bore	0.074 sq. in.
Type of mechanism	Short recoil
Feeding device	Fabric belt
Capacity of feeding device	100–250 rounds
Rate of fire	approx. 450 rpm
Cooling system	Air
Sight radius	13.94 in.
Sear release	9 lb.
Normal pressure	48,000 psi
Trigger pull	7.7 lb.
Ammunition types	Ball, AP, tracer

The M1919 Browning .30 cal. air-cooled medium machine gun was developed from the M1917 water-cooled machine gun of World War I. The M1919 was essentially a company support machine gun requiring a crew of five: a squad leader, the gunner (who carried the tripod and a box of ammunition), an assistant gunner (who carried the gun, a box of ammunition, tools and helped feed the gun during use), and two ammunition carriers. The M1919A4 was mounted on Jeeps, halftracks, armored cars, tanks, amphibious vehicles, and landing craft (LCVP). The presence of this machine gun gave companies additional automatic support fire for assault and defense. The coaxial M37 variant was mounted in armored vehicle turrets next to the main gun and could be belt fed from either side. The 10th Mountain Division utilized this weapon at company level.

M2 .50 Cal. Machine Gun

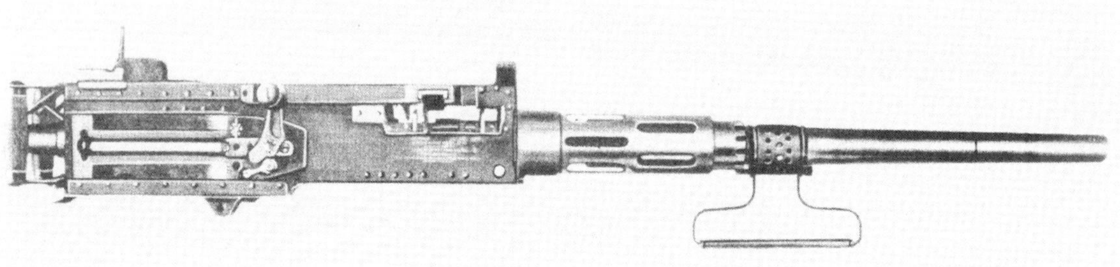

Gun, Machine, Cal. .50, Browning, M2, HB, Flexible (TM 9-2200)	
Weight	84 lb.
Length (overall)	65 in.
Weight of recoiling parts	38.8 lb.
Weight of barrel	29½ lb.
Length of barrel	45 in.
Length of rifling	40.91 in.; 81.8 cal.
Rifling: number of grooves	8
R.H. twist; 1 turn in	30 cal.; 15 in.
Depth of grooves	0.005 in.
Cross-sectional area of bore	0.2021 sq. in.
Type of mechanism	Short recoil
Feeding device	Metallic link belt
Capacity of feeding device	As desired
Rate of fire	450 rpm
Cooling system	Air
Sight radius	20 in.
Firing pin release:	Pressure applied to sear: 10–20 lb.
	Pressure applied to sear slide: 25–35 lb.
Normal pressure	48,000 psi (copper)
Ammunition types	Ball, AP, tracer

M2 Browning .50 cal. machine gun mounted on an 18 in. toboggan with pioneer equipment strapped on. (U.S. Army)

The M2 Browning .50 cal. machine gun ("Ma Deuce") was a heavy machine gun designed by John Browning at the end of World War I. In World War II, it was used against light armored vehicles, infantry, watercraft, fortifications, and aircraft. The M2 was an air-cooled belt-fed machine gun. It fired the .50 BMG (Browning machine gun) cartridge, resulting in long-range, great accuracy, and immense kinetic energy (stopping power). The M2 was a scaled-up version of the M1919 .30 cal. machine gun. The gun was mounted on a tripod when deployed for action.

M20 75 mm Recoilless Rifle

M20 75 mm recoilless rifle mounted on a Weasel. (U.S. Army)

As a result of rapid advances in armor technology during World War II, infantry units and other lightly armed units were highly vulnerable to armored attack. This spawned a demand for a weapon light enough to be carried by infantry units but powerful enough to be effective against armor at medium ranges. In 1943, the Ordnance Department Small Arms Division began developing the recoilless rifle. By 1944, the first pilot models of the 75 mm recoilless rifle were being tested. Full production began in March 1945, and guns were delivered to the European and Pacific Theaters. The advantage of recoilless guns lies in their light weight and relatively high performance. By design, the breach expels propellant gasses rearward, thereby balancing the forces caused by the projectile accelerating out of the gun tube. This eliminated the need for heavy gun mounts, which were a significant part of the weight of a typical artillery piece. A Jeep or weapons carrier could easily carry the M20 recoilless rifle using the standard M1917A1 .30 cal. machine-gun tripod mount. Unfortunately, the recoilless rifle mounted on a Weasel presented a high profile with little protection for the crew and was not adopted by the 10th Mountain Division. This was an infantry-carried weapon used under cover of the terrain.

Technical Data 75 mm Recoilless Rifle, M20 (TM 9-314)	
Length	6 ft. 10 in.
Weight	114½ lb.
Rifling	Uniform, right hand, 1 turn in 22 cal.
Breech	Interrupted screw
Muzzle velocity	1,000 ft./sec. (H.E.A.T. round)
Projectile weight	3.19 lb. (HEAT, shaped charge)
Armor penetration	4 in.

M2 60 mm Mortar

M2 60 mm mortar. (Wikimedia Commons)

The U.S. Army investigated the development of a small mortar as a light infantry support weapon. French engineer Edgar Brandt's design was standardized as mortar, 60 mm M2. An order for 1,500 was placed in January 1940. The mortar squad included a squad leader, a gunner, an assistant gunner, and two ammunition carriers. The weight of the mortar was 42 lb., the caliber 60 mm (2.36 in.), and it could fire 18 rounds per minute with a muzzle velocity of 520 ft./sec. A mortar is a lightweight artillery piece that can provide a significant punch with just a few soldiers as crew. A mortar squad's members were often called "plumbers" as the mortar tube is essentially a pipe. Mortar squads were part of a weapons platoon in the 10th Mountain Division. Sergeant Bill Kennedy designed a simplified sight for the 60 mm mortar that allowed the mortar to be deployed more quickly than the conventional sight. The sight was used in combat in Italy but not adopted by the U.S. Army.

M1 81 mm mortar. (Wikimedia Commons)

2.36 in. Rocket Launcher (Bazooka)

View of first-pattern 1941 M1 bazooka. This antitank weapon could defeat tank armor of 4½ in. at 700 yd. (Wikimedia Commons)

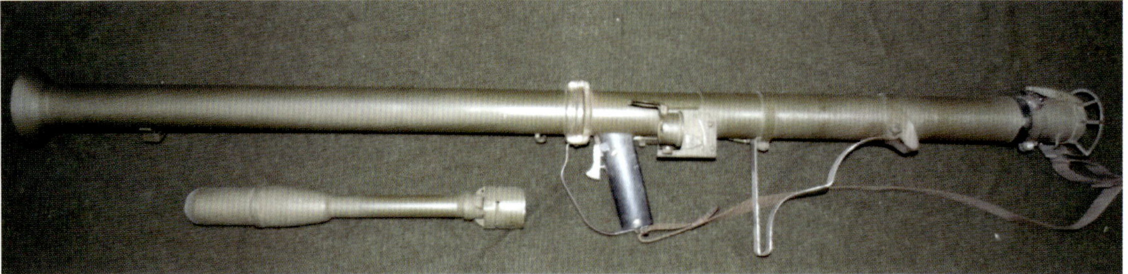

Right-side view of an M9A1 bazooka late-war design with longer tube. It could be split into two tubes for ease of carrying.

At the top of photo: 2.36 in. M6A1 rocket, early war. At the bottom: 2.36 in. M6A3 rocket, late war.

The bazooka, named after a musical instrument invented by Bob Burns, featured high maneuverability, light weight, a rocket-propelled round, and a shaped charge. The shaped charge channeled the explosive into a narrow jet that could penetrate several inches of armor. It was intended to be used by a crew of two infantry soldiers, one being the gunner, the other the loader. The bazooka began development in World War I under the tutelage of Robert Goddard, the father of rocketry, at Worcester Polytechnic Institute in Worcester, Massachusetts. The prototype tube-launched rocket worked well, but the war had ended and the project was canceled. When World War II was underway, there was renewed interest in the development of the bazooka. The M1 bazooka was the first rocket launcher, essentially a tube with a firing mechanism. This developed into the M9A1 bazooka, which could be split into two sections for ease of carrying and had magneto ignition instead of battery ignition.

Bazooka optical sight with range elevation graduations. The firing handle shows a fire and safe selection. Pulling the trigger activates a magneto, which sends current to the rocket, causing a launch.

Vehicles Adopted and/or Tested by the 10th Mountain Division in World War II

Like other divisions in World War II, the 10th Mountain Division was supplied with several vehicles germane to their mission. Vehicles tested to determine their utility for the mission of the 10th Mountain Division included the M7 Snow Tractor, the M36 Snow Tractor, the Eliason Motor Toboggan, the T27 Snow Mobile, the T28 Snow Tractor, the T30 Snow Tractor, the T26 Sno-Cat, and the Crosley Pup, which were not adopted by the 10th. Also tested were the M28 Weasel Carrier, the M29 Weasel Carrier, the M29C Weasel Carrier, and the Jeep, which were used in combat by the 10th. The Weasel handled very well in the snow and the mountains. It was used overseas in Italy to move troops and equipment over mountain roads and ridges. The Jeep was used as an all-purpose vehicle on roadways for hauling equipment and transporting high-ranking officers and wounded soldiers.

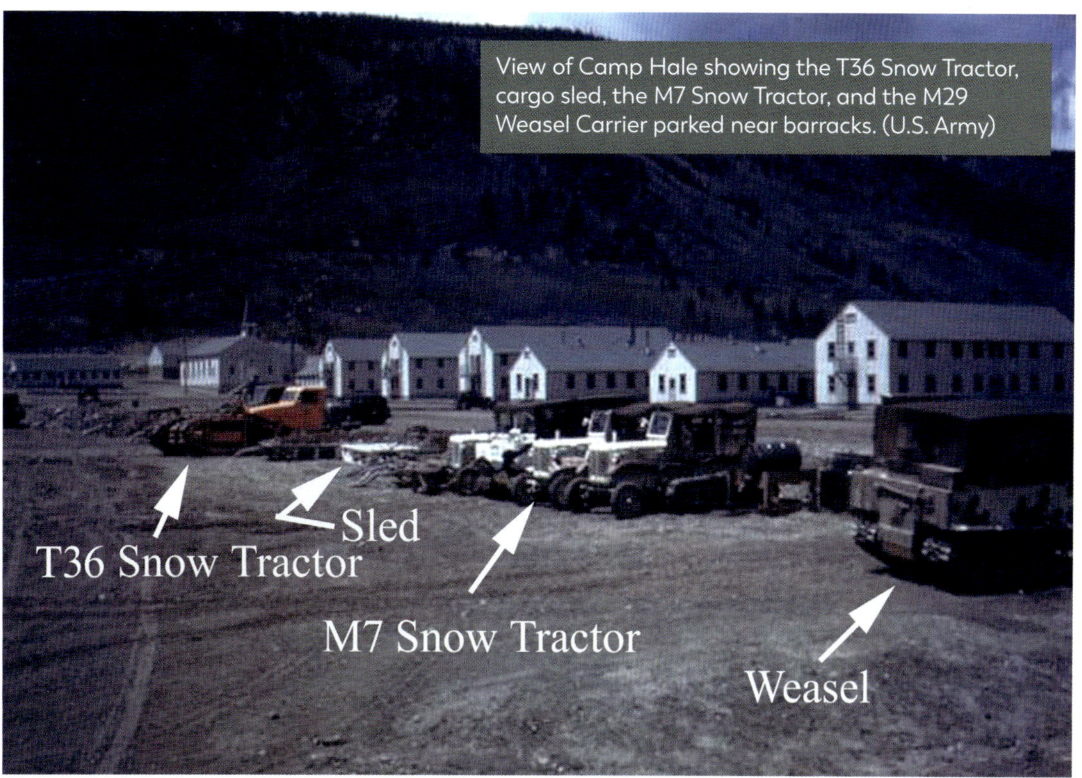

View of Camp Hale showing the T36 Snow Tractor, cargo sled, the M7 Snow Tractor, and the M29 Weasel Carrier parked near barracks. (U.S. Army)

The M28 Weasel

Fear of German development of the atomic bomb gripped Allied strategists in 1942. In April 1940, the Germans invaded Norway and captured the Vemork Norsk Hydroelectric Plant outside Rjukan, the first commercially producing heavy water plant. Heavy water is water with a few more hydrogen atoms added, which act as a moderator to slow down neutrons in nuclear reactions. Scientists considered heavy water to be vital for the nuclear reactors used to make fissionable material for nuclear weapons. Allied top-secret command devised a plan to destroy the heavy water plants. It was proposed that a raid be conducted against the power plants using a highly mobile, snow tractor-like vehicle. The top-secret Project Weasel was initiated, resulting in a highly mobile series of cargo carriers. British inventor Geoffrey Pyke proposed a carrier vehicle that could transport commando troops of the American-Canadian 1st Special Service Force and their equipment for attacking German industrial operations in Norway.

The problem was that no vehicle was available to adequately transport troops and supplies over snow to attack the hydroelectric plant. This gave rise to the design of the Weasel in 1942. Operation *Plough* was conceived as the plan to airdrop Allied forces with over 2,000 troops equipped with over-the-snow vehicles, primarily the Weasel, which would be dropped using a parachute from the belly of a Lancaster bomber.

The U.S. Army Ordnance Department charged the Studebaker Corporation to design and deliver a prototype of the Weasel. Studebaker delivered their first prototype in less than 40 days after approval. Their design was 16 ft. in length, which was considered too long. The U.S. Army Ordnance Department accepted a new design, which was 11 ft. in length and was designated T15. In late 1942, the T15 was standardized as Light Cargo Carrier M28 with a total production of 766 vehicles plus 80 sleds. Parachute airdrop testing of the M28 from under the belly of a C-54 cargo plane was successful.

As the war progressed, Operation *Plough* was canceled as the hydroelectric plant was put out of commission by the Norwegian Resistance and British bombing. It became clear that the Weasel could play a role in transporting equipment in other units. The only use of the M28 was in the Kiska attack in the Aleutian

M28 Weasels at Camp Hale, Colorado. The M28 Weasel, the first of the Weasel designs, had four canted road wheels on each side, which tended to throw tracks during turns. Later models had eight pairs of non-canted road wheels on each side, with a track guide between each pair. A front-mounted engine replaced the rear engine, which improved the vehicle's balance. (U.S. Army)

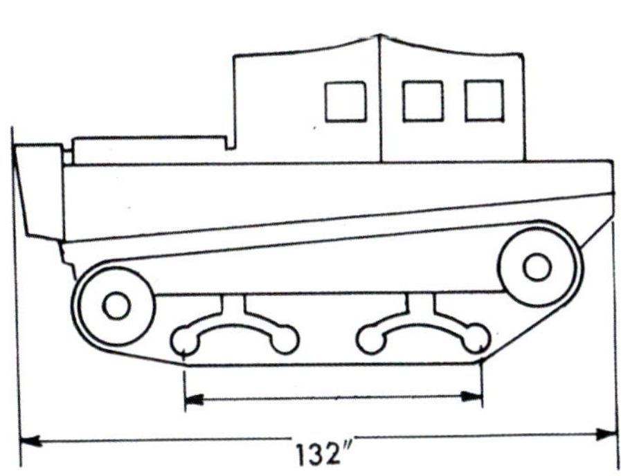

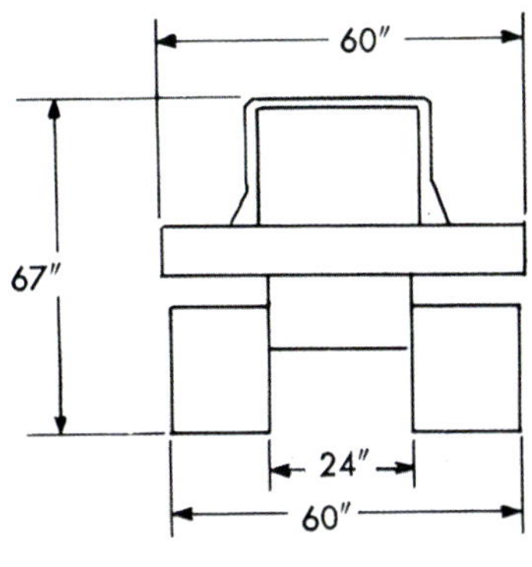

Generic side and front view drawings of the M28 Weasel with measurements. The vehicle was originally 192 in. long but was reduced to 132 in. (TM 9-2800)

Islands in Alaska by the 87th Regiment from Camp Hale. The wide tracks had very low ground pressure, allowing the vehicle to operate efficiently in the snow. Although the seating capacity in an M28 was limited, it could tow several troops on skis, like the sport of skijoring.

The light carrier's potential was recognized and utilized in many theaters, such as Europe, the Pacific, and Alaska. The 10th Mountain Division used Weasels for training in Colorado, the 87th Infantry Regiment from Camp Hale used Weasels in the Kiska operation in the Aleutian Islands, and the 10th Mountain Division used Weasels in Italy. Studebaker Corporation of South Bend, Indiana, manufactured the vehicle. The first Weasel was the T15, later designated T28 Cargo Carrier, with 15 in.-wide tracks attached to a steel reinforced rubber band. The vehicle had to be lightweight and droppable by parachute. The early production models were designated M28, while the later versions were the M29 and M29C (convertible to amphibious usage).

Weasel with experimental gun mount for a Browning M2 .50 cal. machine gun. This gun mount was never adopted by the 10th.

M28 Weasel top view showing two seats and relatively limited cargo capacity. The ski poles and snowshoes are on top of the engine compartment. (John Adams-Graf)

The M28 had an engine mounted in the rear, driving a differential and track sprocket drive in the front of the vehicle. The vehicle had a two-passenger capacity. The M28 Weasel was tail-heavy since the engine was in the back and tended to throw tracks. The orientation of the road wheels and the elasticity of the steel cable-reinforced track resulted in the track climbing over the road wheels and drive sprockets during turns. These design-related problems were demonstrated during the usage of the M28. The vehicle was redesigned and designated T24 with a front-mounted engine, a rear-mounted drive axle, a larger cargo compartment, a strengthened suspension system, and more robust road wheels. The T24 was standardized as Cargo Carrier M29 in late 1943.

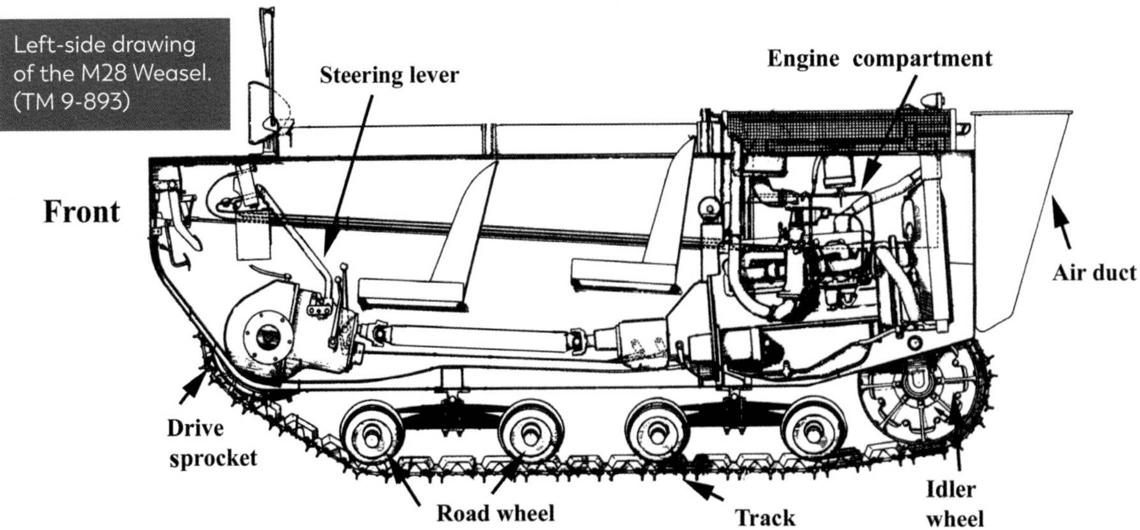

Left-side drawing of the M28 Weasel. (TM 9-893)

A – Rear cargo box	B – Engine compartment	C – Exhaust muffler guard
D – Demolition timer control	E – Radio	F – Cargo area
G – Exterior armament	H – Demolition case	J – Driver's seat
K – Windshield bumper & clamp	L – Electric windshield wiper	M – Towing eye
N – Manual windshield wiper	P – Spotlight guard	Q – Spotlight
R – Ski rack	S – Drive shaft cover	T – Rear seat
U – Front engine compartment	V – Gas cap	W – Rear marker light
X – Rear air duct		

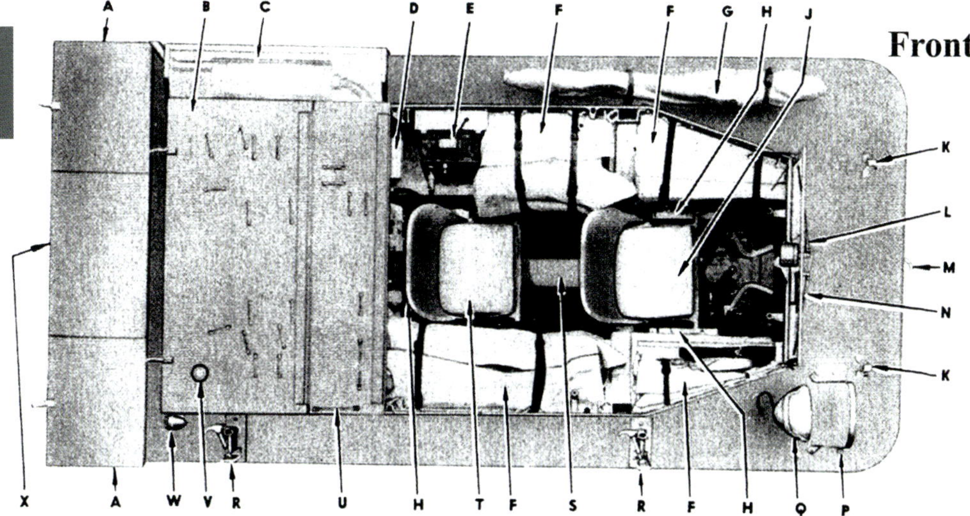

Top view of the M28 Weasel. (TM 9-893)

Right front view of an M28 Weasel showing white canvas top with clear, flexible plastic windows. (John Adams-Graf)

M28 Weasel at Camp Hale towing a cargo sled. A cargo sled was an absolute necessity for hauling heavy equipment since the M28 had limited space and weight capacity. The M28, like other Weasels, was a prime mover for towing sleds and skiers. (John Adams-Graf)

Left front view of an M28 Weasel. (John Adams-Graf)

M28 Weasels of the 87th Regiment of the 10th Mountain Division on the northern shore of Kiska Island. Supplies from ships were loaded onto these Weasels and transported to the 87th's camp. This was the first instance of the usage of Weasels in a combat area. (U.S. Army)

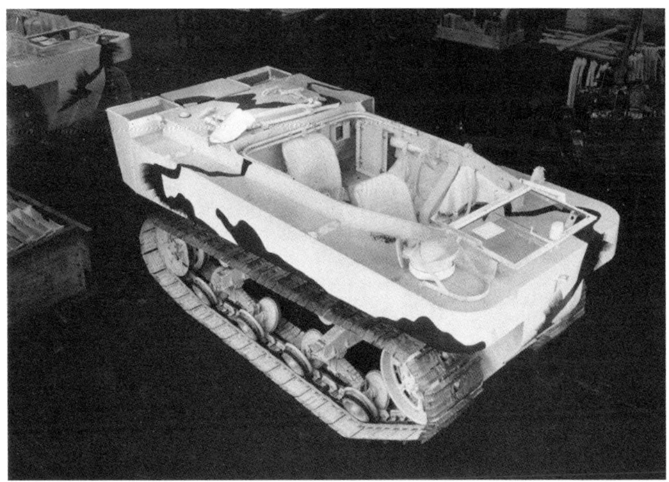

M28 Weasel right front view. The road wheels are canted inward in this design, which was changed to vertical wheels in later models. The number of road wheels was then doubled to reduce the propensity for throwing a track. (John Adams-Graf)

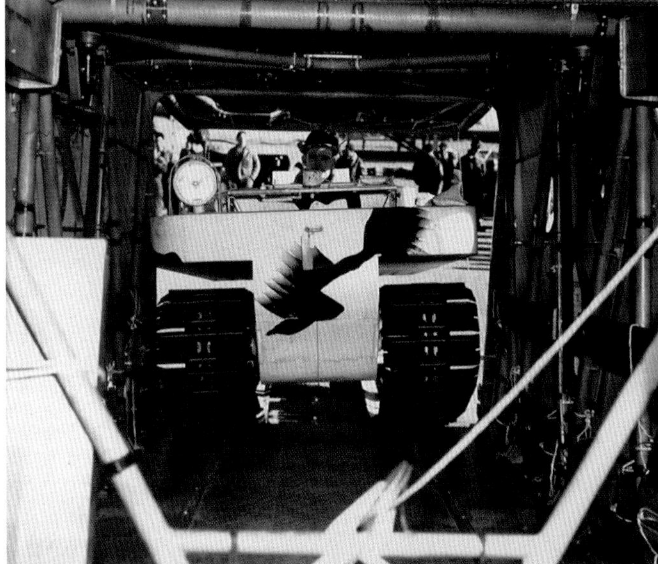

M28 Weasel front view, inside a glider. It was a requirement that the Weasel could be delivered by air, such as by parachute, under the belly of a Lancaster bomber, or by glider. (John Adams-Graf)

M28 Weasel rear view, inside a glider. (John Adams-Graf)

M29 Weasel

In 1943, the redesigned Weasel appeared at Aberdeen Proving Grounds. The M29 Weasel was an improvement over the M28: it was wider and had the engine in the front and drive sprockets at the rear. It had more cargo capacity and three seats in the rear for personnel. The road wheels on the M29 were vertical, while those of the M28 were canted at an angle. Approximately 4,476 M29 cargo carriers were manufactured by Studebaker in 1943 and 1944. The first 3,312 vehicles were painted white/black camo, while the rest were olive drab.

The vehicle performed well in various terrains and was used in combat in Italy, Western Europe, and the Pacific. An improvement to the flotation capability of the M29 was the M29C, which had floating cells attached to the bow and stern of the vehicle to allow amphibious operation. The tracks propelled the M29C in the water, and twin rudders in the stern steered the vehicle. A capstan (winch) was provided in the bow for recovery operations.

In the spring of 1944, all Weasels manufactured were of the M29C model. When the flotation cells on the M29C were removed, it was basically the same as the M29. Some 10,647 M29C Weasels were manufactured for the U.S. Army in 1944 and 1945. The M29C was used in combat in Western Europe from January 1945 and in the Pacific from December 1944. The Ford Motor Company was also considered for manufacturing the Weasel. However, the Studebaker Company was keeping up with demand, and the war was starting to wind down, making it unnecessary to engage another manufacturer. The Weasel proved useful for supply and transport because of its ability to traverse rugged terrain which other vehicles could not. It could pull cargo trailers and sleds and tow a squad of mountain troops on skis with two tow ropes.

The standard automotive Studebaker Champion, 6-cylinder, water-cooled gasoline engine powered the M29 and M29C. A clutch plate transmitted power via a propeller shaft to the rear differential unit. The transmission was three speed plus reverse with a high- and low-range selector. The vehicle had two tracks with 56 metal rubberized grousers approximately 20 in. wide attached to steel cable-reinforced rubber belts. The grousers would engage the sprocket drive at the vehicle's rear, propelling the tracks. The suspension consisted of four transverse springs with 16 pairs of road wheels to carry the vehicle's load. Track tension was adjusted at the front idler wheels, where the idler axles could be moved fore or aft to adjust the tension. The hull was a watertight sheet metal tub with five drain plugs. Two watertight float cells were attached to the bow and stern of the vehicle for flotation and amphibious operation. The bow cell had a hatch for stowage and a splash guard to reduce the chance of water entering the engine compartment. Since the tracks provided the propulsion, aprons were placed next to the upper section of the tracks to facilitate forward motion through the water.

Prototype M29 Weasel designated T24 at Aberdeen Proving Grounds. (John Adams-Graf)

Specifications for the M29 and M29C (TM 9-772)	
Crew	2–4
Length overall	
M29 with pintle hook and towing eye	125¾ in.
M29 without pintle hook	120¼ in.
M29C to end of rudders, surf guard lowered	192⅛ in.
M29C to end of hull, surf guard lowered	177⅛ in.
Width	
M29 (15 in. track)	61 in.
M29 (20 in. track)	66 in.
M29C	67¼ in.
Height overall (with top and bows)	70 13/16 in.
Weight (net)	
M29 (15 in. track)	3,725 lb.
M29C	4,771 lb.
Crew and equipment	1,200 lb.
Weight (gross)	
M29 (15 in. track)	4,925 lb.
M29 (20 in. track)	5,277 lb.
M29C	5,971 lb.
Maximum towed load	3,800 lb.
Ground clearance	11 in.
Tread (center-to-center of tracks)	45 in.
Length of track on ground	78⅛ in.
Number of track shoes	2 × 56
Ground pressure	
M29 (15 in. track)	approx. 2.10 psi
M29 (20 in. track)	approx. 1.69 psi
M29C	approx. 1.91 psi
Top speeds	
Short periods	4,000 rpm
Sustained	3,600 rpm
Top speed in calm water (M29C)	4 mph
Cruising range on roads	175 mi.

T24 Weasel towing a cargo sled. The official towing capacity of the Weasel was approximately 3,800 lb. The ability to tow a sled depends on the ski/snow friction. The load of 3,800 lb. could be easy to tow on hard, slippery snow but hard on deep, heavy, wet snow. (John Adams-Graf)

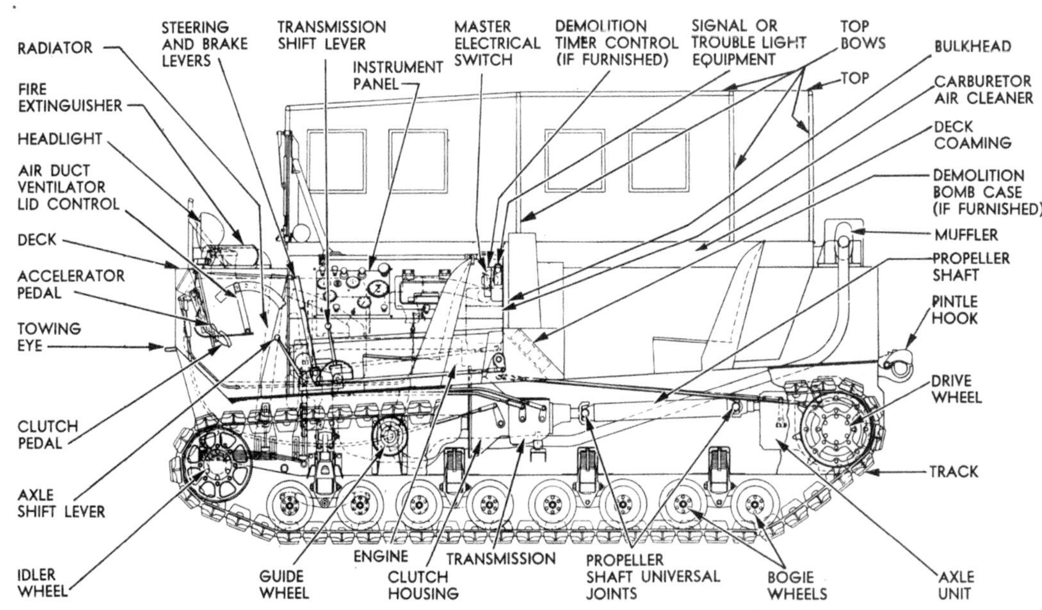

Side-view drawing of the M29. (TM 9-772)

The M29C was essentially the same as an M29 except for having a means of attaching float cells to the bow and stern. The Weasel had connections to attach a front and rear float cell, making the vehicle amphibious for light sea conditions only, such as inland waterways. The freeboard was low, and swamping was a concern in heavy seas. Twin rudders were on the stern cell, and propulsion was essentially from the track grouser, resulting in a relatively low speed of about 3 to 4 mph. The M29C was used extensively by the 10th Mountain Division in Italy for hauling supplies and troops over snow-covered mountainous areas and other rough terrain. Weasels with the 10th Mountain Division did not usually use the float cells since other amphibious vehicles,

M29C Weasel without float cells painted in typical 10th Mountain Division camouflage.

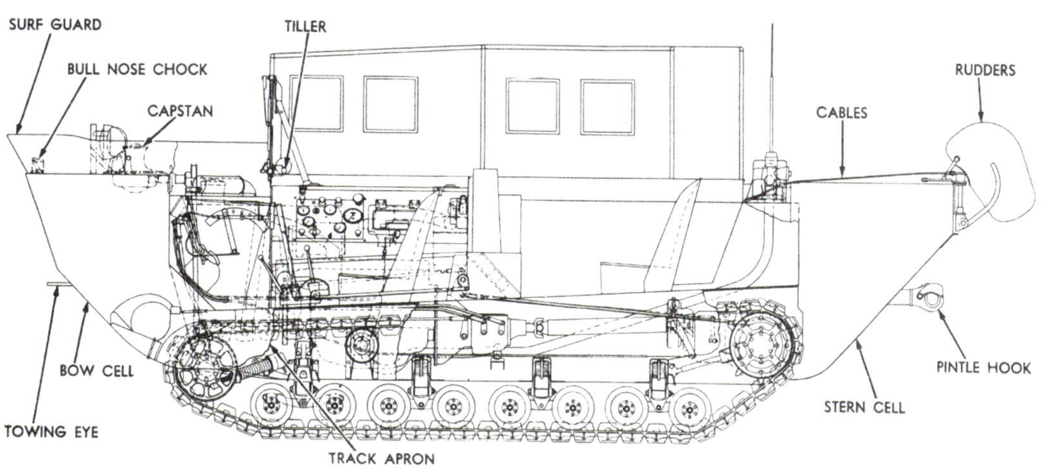

Side-view drawing of the M29C with bow and stern float cells attached. (TM 9-772)

such as the DUKW amphibious truck, were available through transportation companies. The vehicle worked well on the snow, even in powdery-snow conditions. It tended to be slightly top-heavy and would roll over if it approached an embankment at an angle. The driver had to be careful when pivoting on rough ground because of the propensity to throw a track.

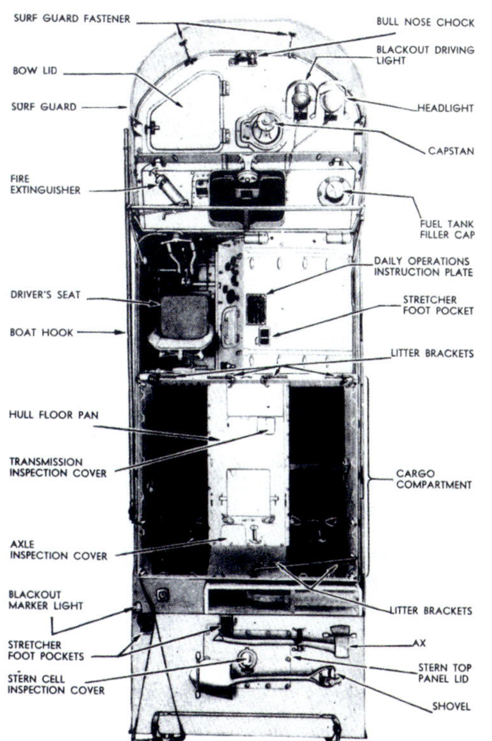

Top view of the M29C Weasel. (TM 9-772)

View of driver's compartment on an M29C Weasel. There were three forward speeds and one reverse, with high and low range. The tall steering levers were connected to the brakes. Pulling on the right lever made the vehicle turn right, and pulling on the left lever turned the vehicle left. Pulling both levers stopped the vehicle.

Left rear view of an M29C test vehicle. The front and rear flotation cells were bolted to the hull and could be quickly installed or removed. Twin rudders aided in steering, and an apron placed on the sides near the upper track sections helped increase the forward thrust from the tracks, which gave a speed of 4 mph in calm water. The tracks did not provide enough forward thrust in windy conditions to make headway. The Weasel equipped with float cells was not intended for heavy seas. (Studebaker Proving Grounds)

M29C Weasel with bow and stern float cells installed. Members of the Women's Army Corps (WAC) from the 7th Service Command are standing in front of a Weasel. (John Adams-Graf)

View of rear seats in an M29C. Some seats were white to match the white camouflage, while others were olive drab to match the olive-drab color.

M29 or M29C Weasels ferrying 10th soldiers and equipment over a ridge near Monte Grande d'Aiano, Italy. The float cells could easily be removed from an M29C, making it look like an M29. A 2½-ton truck and WC51 Weapons Carrier are also shown (and are discussed in the next chapter). (National Archives)

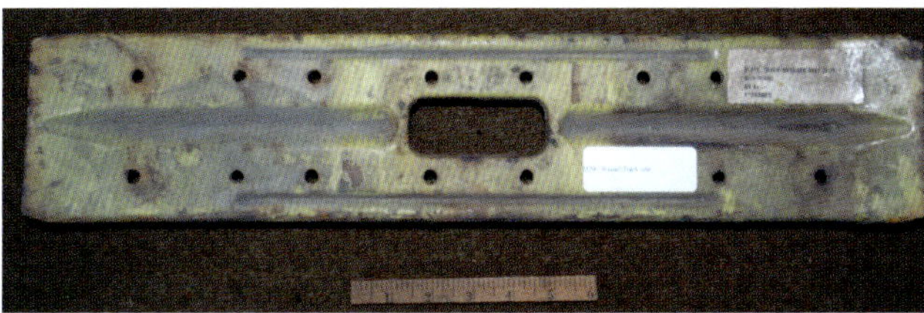

Weasel 20 in. track section, top view. The track is bolted to the reinforced rubber bands around the track.

The bottom view of the Weasel 20 in. track section shows the rubberized undercoating of the track. Two rubber track pads lifted the vehicle about ½ in. above the grouser blade when traveling on concrete or asphalt to avoid wearing out the grouser blade.

M7 Snow Tractor

Restored M7 Snow Tractor serial number 283.

M7 Snow Tractor at Camp Hale.

The Allis Chalmers farm tractor company designed the M7 (T26E4) Snow Tractor at a request from the Army Air Corps for a vehicle to rescue downed pilots in remote areas. The front of the vehicle resembled that of Allis Chalmers' farm tractors. The vehicle was standardized in August 1943 but reduced to a limited standard in November 1944.

The driver's compartment shows the instrument panel, shifter, and foot pedals. Foot pedals placed on each side would lock the track on one side, making it easier to turn. The transmission was three speeds forward and one in reverse, with high or low range selected. The engine and transmission were the same as the World War II Jeep. The driver's compartment was cramped, making it difficult for anyone over 6 ft. tall to fit.

The U.S. Army required that existing components of other vehicles be used to reduce the spare parts inventory. Willys MB Jeep powertrain components such as a Jeep engine, transmission, and rear differential were used. The M7 was essentially a halftrack with the front wheels easily removable and replaced with skis. The track consisted of two rubber belts with four steel cables molded into the rubber on each belt. It was, unfortunately, easy to throw a track on this vehicle. The track plates were 18 in. wide and looked like the Weasel track. The brakes on the tracks were independent to increase maneuverability. The road wheels had a small rolling radius, resulting in severe shock loads. The small road wheels also caused significant bearing wear. Consequently, when operating, greasing road wheel bearings was necessary almost daily, which was a maintenance headache. The transmission was the same as the Jeep, and a standard Jeep engine, which was underpowered for this application, supplied power. The M7 was tested at Camp Hale and was shown to be inadequate for the 10th Mountain Division's needs. The troop- or cargo-carrying capacity was inadequate unless the vehicle towed a sled that contained the cargo. Several mechanical problems still had to be solved. The total production by Allis Chalmers was 291 vehicles.

Left-side view of an M7 Snow Tractor with top and side curtains installed. The skis were stored over the wheels and appeared to look like fenders. When the skis were deployed, a keel at the back lower surface aided in turning the vehicle and acted as a guard when riding over hard terrain or rocks.

Skis deployed and front tires still attached. Although the front tires could be removed, this configuration made it easy to travel through snow and over dry ground. Turning the steering wheel steered the vehicle adequately on land and in snow. There was usually no need to lock a track to aid in turning. The vehicle was a combination of Jeep and Allis Chalmers parts.

Ordnance testing of the M7 Snow Tractor, May 5, 1944. All covers are on the vehicle, including the occupant compartment top, a hood cover to keep the engine warm, and a radiator cover to allow the engine to run warmer in arctic weather. Hot air from the engine infiltrates through the firewall, heating the occupant compartment. For cold starts, the engine was equipped with a fuel primer and a choke. (U.S. Army)

M7 Snow Tractor and M19 Snow Trailer being tested at Aberdeen Proving Grounds. (U.S. Army)

M7 Snow Tractor and M19 Snow Trailer without the canvas top. The M7 relied on sleds for hauling cargo since the vehicle's carrying capacity was limited. (John Adams-Graf)

M7 Snow Tractor and M19 Snow Trailer at a test area at Aberdeen Proving Grounds. (U.S. Army)

M7 Specifications (TM 9-774)	
Wheelbase (with wheels)	81 in.
Length, overall (with wheels)	10 ft. 11 in.
Width, overall (with skis)	5 ft. 3 in.
Width, overall (with wheels)	5 ft. 3 in.
Height, overall (with skis)	5 ft. 3½ in.
Height, overall (with wheels)	5 ft. 4 in.
Wheel size	15 in.
Tire size	4.00 × 15 in.
Tire type	Rib type
Tread (center to center) (with wheels)	
Front	51 11/16 in.
Rear	45 in.
Tread (center to center) (with skis)	
Front	40 in.
Rear	45 in.
Crew	2
Weight of vehicle: empty	2,620 lb.
Weight of vehicle: with personnel	3,120 lb.
Ground pressure (skis)	1.1 psi
Ground pressure (tracks on snow)	¾ psi
Ground contact area (with skis)	3,348 sq. in.
Ground clearance (with skis)	12¾ in.
Ground clearance (with wheels)	13¾ in.
Pintle height	15¾ in.
Type and grade of fuel (octane rating)	Gasoline, 68 octane (min.)
Approach angle (with skis)	40°
Approach angle (with wheels)	60°
Departure angle (with wheels or skis)	60°
Maximum allowable speed (low range)	
1st gear	4 mph
2nd gear	7 mph
3rd gear	10 mph
Reverse gear	3 mph

Maximum allowable speed (high range)	
1st gear	15 mph
2nd gear	26 mph
3rd gear	41 mph
Reverse gear	11 mph
Minimum turning radius (right)	15 ft.
(left)	15 ft.
Fording depth	30 in.
Maximum drawbar pull	1,000 lb.
Maximum grade ascending ability	75%
Maximum allowable engine speed	4,000 rpm
Fuel consumption (at 20 mph without load)	15 mpg
Cruising range (at 20 mph without load)	160 mi.
Transmission capacity	¾ qt.
Auxiliary transmission capacity	¾ qt.
Differential case capacity	1¼ qt.
Fuel tank capacity	10½ gal.
Cooling system capacity	3 gal.
Crankcase capacity	5 qt.

M19 Snow Trailer

The M19 Snow Trailer was designed to be towed by the M7 Snow Tractor. The M19 trailer weighed 640 lb. and had a load capacity of 2,000 lb. A tubing steel frame, to be covered with canvas, supported a wooden body with side panels that supported bows. The pintle hitch for the M7 and M19 was unique and did not fit on other vehicles, such as the Jeep. The trailer was to carry cargo for the 10th Mountain Division.

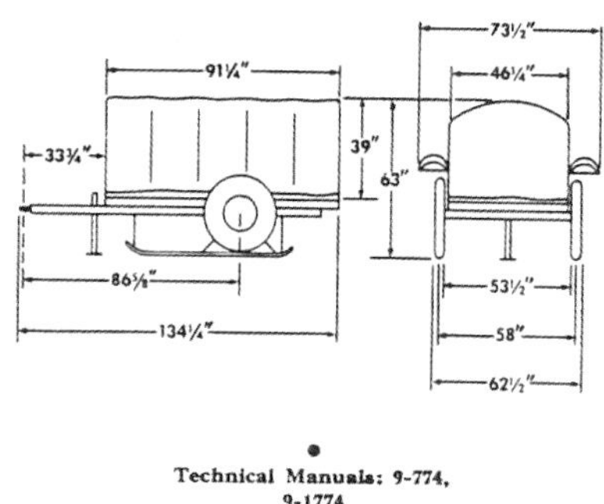

M19 Snow Trailer. (TM 9-774)

M19 Snow Trailer. (U.S. Army)

T19 Snow Trailer at Detroit Arsenal for testing. Tires with a drive tread were unnecessary for a trailer because traction was unnecessary. Earlier, trailers and towed gun carriages used ordinary truck tires. (U.S. Army)

Left-side view of M19 Snow Trailer showing closeup view of the ski. (John Adams-Graf)

Approximately 600 trailers were manufactured during World War II. The lightness of the trailer construction resulted in several weak points when loaded to 2,000 lb. The bed of the trailer would deform if loaded away from the axle. The tow frame was fabricated from tubing, and the lack of internal coating made the unit subject to corrosion-related failure. The wheels were ordinary MB/GPW split combat rims. An M7 could tow two trailers on level ground but had difficulty towing two over rough ground. When rough ground was encountered, it was traversed one trailer at a time. Since the 10th Mountain Division did not adopt the M7 Snow Tractor, neither was the M19 Snow Trailer adopted because it was designed primarily to be towed by the M7.

M36 Snow Tractor

Three M36 snow tractors were purchased and sent to Camp Hale for testing. They were manufactured by the Iron Fireman Company, which manufactured automatic stokers for furnaces. Early T36 models had a two-person, later enlarged to a three-person, cab, as shown in the photos. A 6-cylinder Dodge flat-head T224 military engine (99 hp at 3,300 rpm) was installed in the vehicle, along with a 4-speed transmission.

Borg & Beck manufactured the clutch. The driveshaft was connected to a controlled differential, which drove the rear sprocket by a roller chain. The controlled differential was a Celtrac, model MG, planetary steering differential, which continuously applied power to both tracks. The track was a rubber conveyor belt with U-channel grousers bolted to the track on the outside and drive lugs bolted on the inside. The tracks were 2 ft. wide, resulting in a ground pressure of 1.73 psi for the 7,500 lb. vehicle. There were 16 road wheels in pivoting

Left-side view of a later-model M36 with three-person cab.

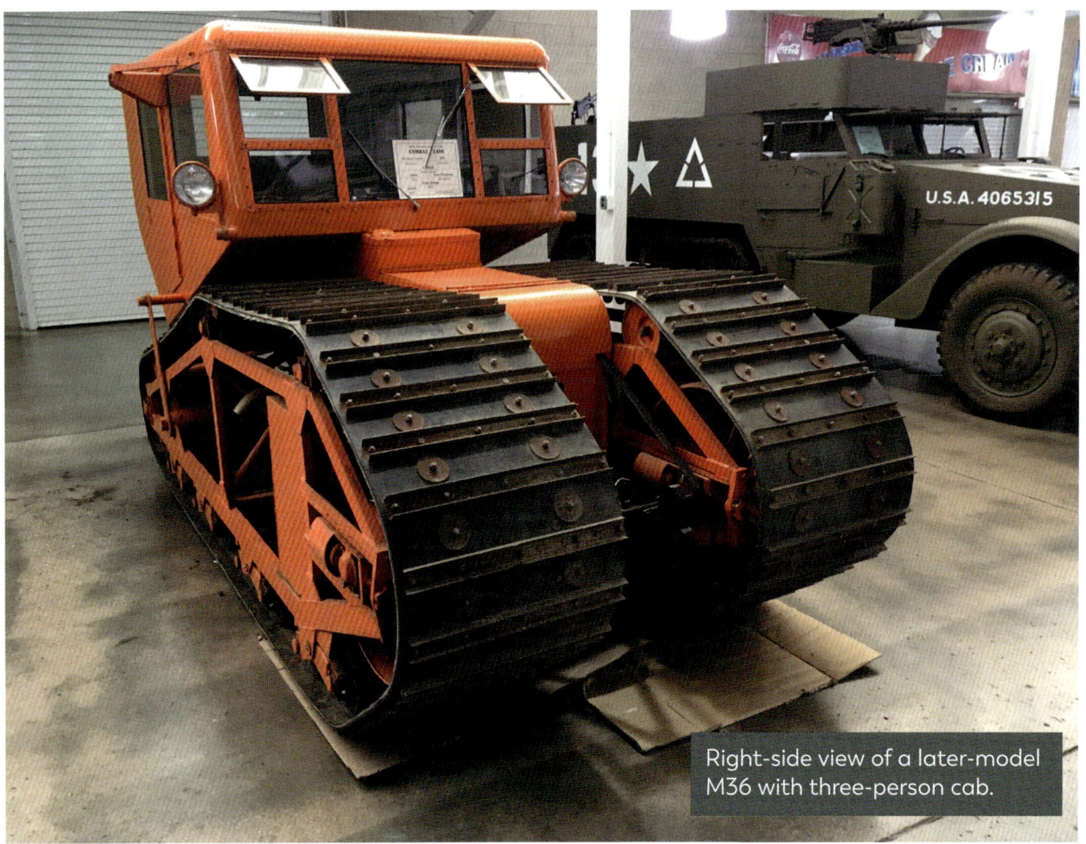

Right-side view of a later-model M36 with three-person cab.

M36 Snow Tractor with three-person cab and independent right and left tracks. (Detroit Arsenal)

pairs but no flexible suspension. Speed was 1.27 mph in low gear and up to 21 mph in high gear. The vehicle was designed to tow a sled but also carry 276 lb. of fuel, 525 lb. of personnel, and 50 lb. of stowed equipment.

The electrical system was 12 volt with enough power to operate a radio such as the SCR-187. The vehicle would not operate in over 2 ft. of soft snow. Above 2 ft. of snow, the vehicle would tend to float on top and lose traction with the ground, making it difficult to travel. The chain drive would accumulate ice and be on the verge of breaking or stretching. The track width rollers at the bottom of the tracks would accumulate snow and bear heavily against the tracks, causing bearing failure. To summarize, this vehicle did not operate well in deep snow. After testing at Camp Hale, this vehicle was not adopted as standard issue for the 10th Mountain Division.

DETROIT ARSENAL
NEG. NO. 8294 DATE 25 July 1941 DEVELOPMENT & ENGINEERING
Three-quarter right front view of Sno-Motor and Sled.

Early model M36 called the Snow Motor with two-man cab. This had a single track and was steered by hydraulic arms connected to the sled. (U.S. Army)

Eliason Motor Toboggan

The 10th Mountain Division command was interested in any mode of transport that could negotiate the variety of snow conditions in the mountain environment. One such vehicle tested was the Eliason Motor Toboggan. The vehicle was approximately 12 ft. long and 3 ft. wide. A 2-cylinder 74 c.i.d. Indian motorcycle engine powered a belt-type track like that used in snowmobiles today. Metal crossbars were attached to the rubber track to grip the snow. The vehicle worked reasonably well in hard snow-pack conditions. However, the vehicle would easily sink in soft, deep snow, and the track would merely spin. Engine power output was reduced at high

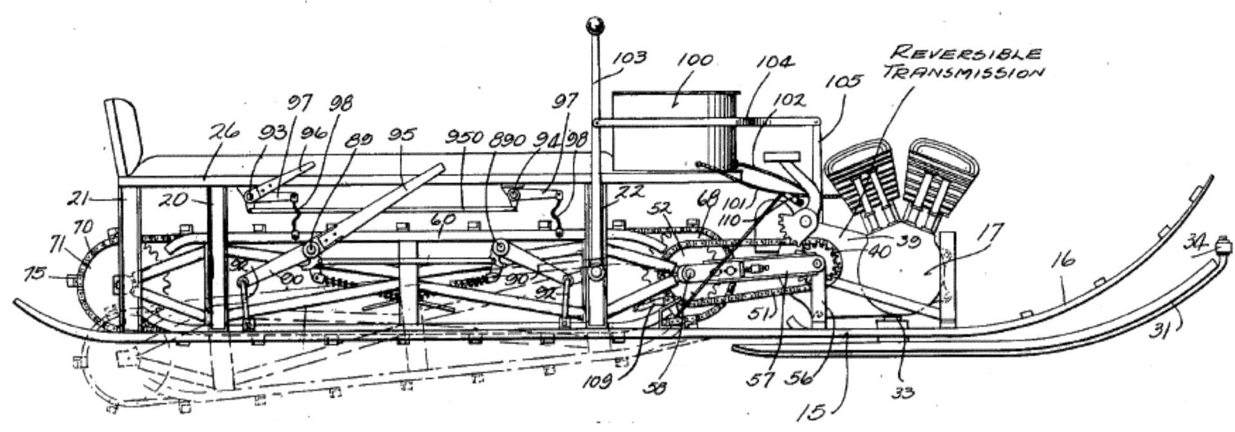

Patent drawing of the Eliason Motorized Toboggan. (U.S. Patent Office)

The Eliason Motorized Toboggan, Model A. (Eskelson)

Skijoring behind an Eliason Motor Toboggan at Camp Hale. (U.S. Army)

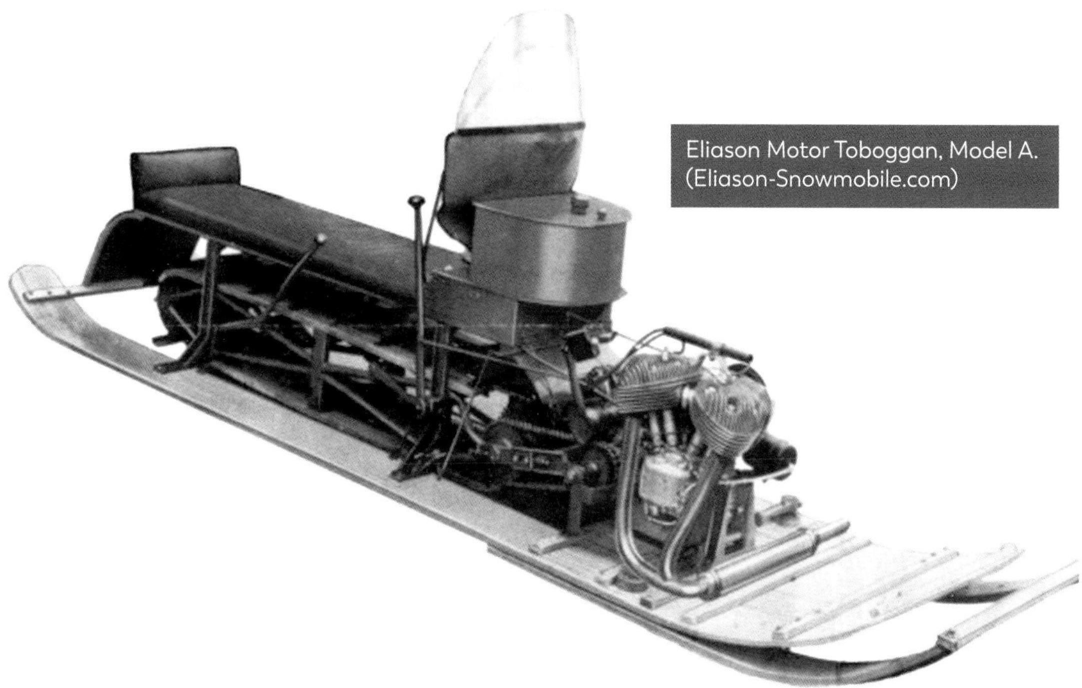

Eliason Motor Toboggan, Model A. (Eliason-Snowmobile.com)

altitudes, so the engine tended to overheat since it operated at maximum rpm due to the high altitude. Attempts at augmented cooling with fans were unsuccessful. Pulling mountain troops on skis (skijoring) and hauling a sled at high altitudes aggravated the overheating problem. This sled was primarily designed for the compacted snow conditions of the Midwest and East, at lower altitudes than the mountains in Colorado. Because of these deficiencies, the Ordnance Department and 10th Mountain Division never adopted the vehicle. Similar sleds met the same fate, but the Ordnance Department did not give up on the concept.

Eliason Motor Toboggan, Model B being tested by a 10th Mountain Division soldier at Camp Hale. (U.S. Army)

T27 Snowmobile

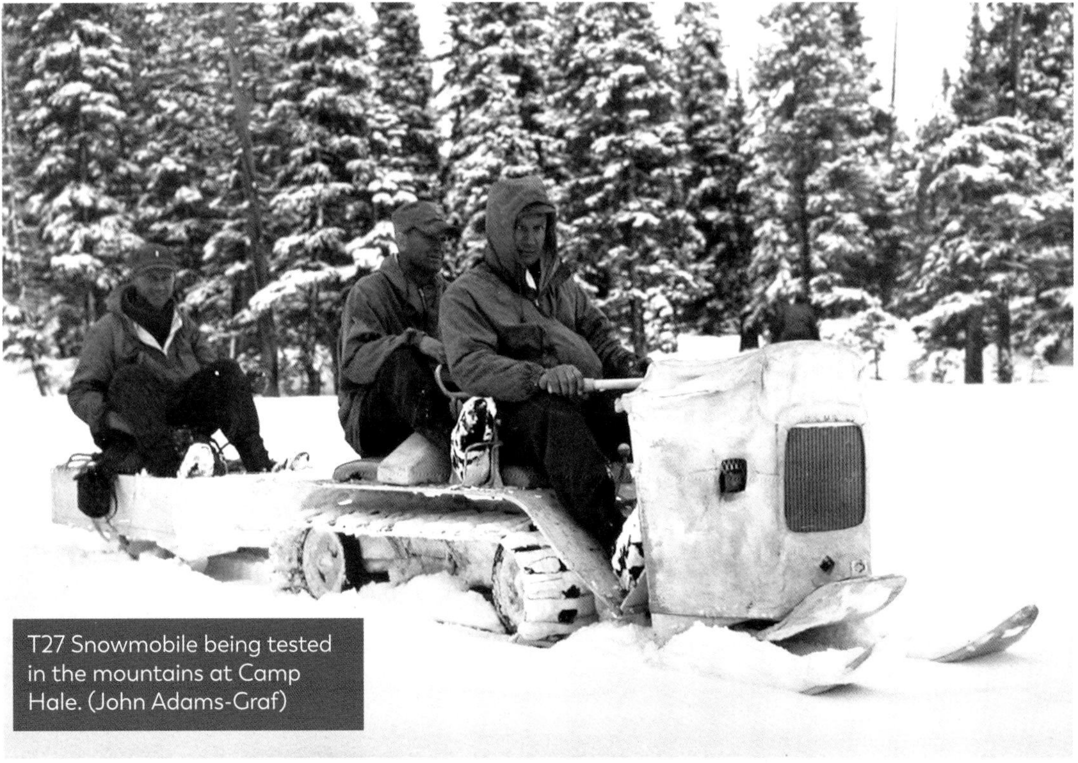

T27 Snowmobile being tested in the mountains at Camp Hale. (John Adams-Graf)

As a result of testing various sleds, such as the Eliason, a set of specifications for the ideal snowmobile was presented for bid:

1. Low center of gravity.
2. Ground pressure along the length of the track should be uniform.
3. The vehicle should be a halftrack design with skis in front.
4. The skis in front should be wide enough to provide good steering in heavy snow.
5. The tracks should operate independently so one can power forward and the other in reverse to allow pivoting.
6. An average ground pressure of 0.7 psi is optimum.
7. Horsepower weight ratio of 60 hp per ton is desirable.
8. Space between tracks should be minimal to allow easier turning in snow.
9. If the space between tracks is 1.4 times the width of a track, then the ground clearance should be at least 22 in.
10. A waterproof electrical system is required.

11. Water should not accumulate in fuel lines.
12. Cold-starting systems such as a fuel primer should be available.
13. It must be as light as possible to make it easy to extricate.

The best design was the T27 Allis Chalmers snowmobile. It was 9 ft. long and 32 in. wide. Twelve in. diameter driving and idler wheels on a 41 in. wheelbase supported and drove the track. There were no road wheels. The middle of the track was pressed against the snow by slider bars. This design did not work well because of the high frictional wear between the track and the slider bars. A motorcycle-type handlebar steered the front 35 in. long skis. The engine was a Waukesha ICK 4 cylinder, generating approximately 22 hp. This engine was considered too heavy for such a sled. Several test vehicles, such as one using an opposed-cylinder Harley Davidson engine, were manufactured with variations and tested at Camp Hale. Overheating of the Harley air-cooled engine resulted from the high power output required, a slow speed, which limited air cooling, and high altitudes that reduced power output. Like other sleds of this design, the T27 did not perform well in deep powder snow because the track could not grab enough snow to propel it forward. The vehicle proved unsatisfactory, and the project was abandoned toward the war's end. Additional modifications to the T27 were the T27E1 and T27E2.

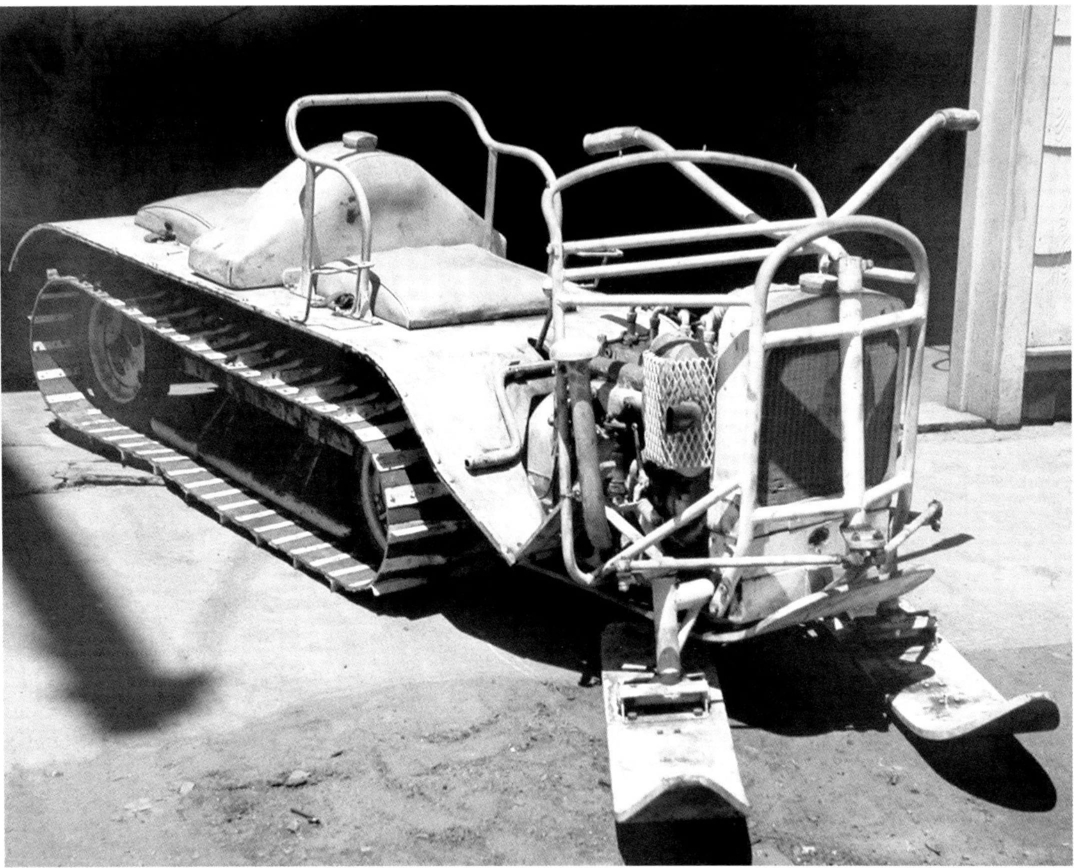

T27 Snowmobile at Camp Hale. (John Adams-Graf)

Snow Tractor T27E1. (John Adams-Graf)

Snow Tractor T27E2 with upgrades to the T27E1. (John Adams-Graf)

T28 Snow Tractor

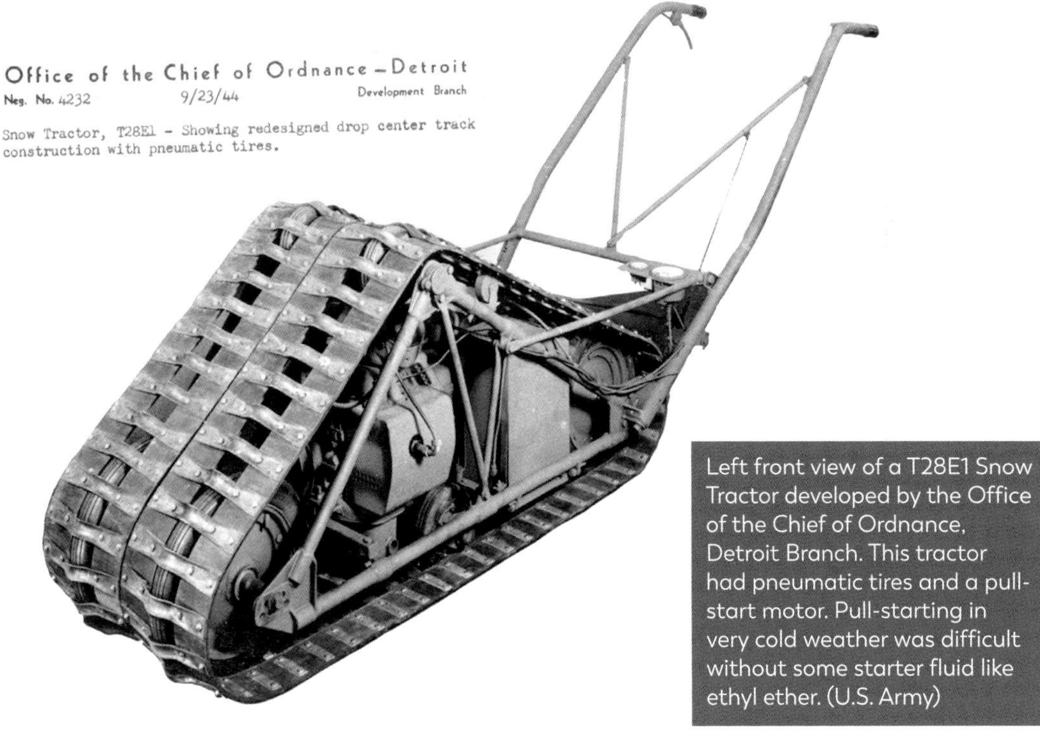
Office of the Chief of Ordnance – Detroit
Neg. No. 4232 9/23/44 Development Branch
Snow Tractor, T28E1 - Showing redesigned drop center track construction with pneumatic tires.

Left front view of a T28E1 Snow Tractor developed by the Office of the Chief of Ordnance, Detroit Branch. This tractor had pneumatic tires and a pull-start motor. Pull-starting in very cold weather was difficult without some starter fluid like ethyl ether. (U.S. Army)

Left rear view of a T28E1 Snow Tractor. The 10th Mountain Division did not adopt this snow tractor. (U.S. Army)

T30 Snow Tractor

Snow Tractor T30 with M31 pedestal mount with 30 cal. machine gun, September 23, 1944. The gunner is vulnerable in this design. The 10th Mountain Division did not adopt this vehicle. (U.S. Army)

T26 Sno-Cat

Tucker Sno-Cat T26 illustrates the wheel and ski attachment design. The 10th Mountain Division did not adopt this vehicle. (U.S. Army)

Early Tucker T26 Sno-Cat. (U.S. Army)

The T26 Tucker Sno-Cat was developed in the early 1940s by Mr. E. M. Tucker. It became one of the most popular snow vehicles and was used in several ski areas after the war. The vehicle featured a track that rolled around two pontoons and was driven by a rear differential. The front had wheels and skis for steering. The vehicle worked well in the snow but was plagued by maintenance problems. The track would wear and it was difficult to tighten. Several steel rollers in the pontoon supported the vehicle on the track. These rollers were small in diameter and would turn very fast when the vehicle was traveling at about 20 mph, which resulted in increased bearing wear. Since the rollers were at the bottom of the pontoon, they collected mud and debris, resulting in bearing failure. Because of inadequate bearing shaft seals, Tucker produced his own seals. However, the bearings still required periodic greasing, which was a maintenance problem since they were located at the bottom of the pontoon and were often full of mud. This vehicle worked well in the postwar period with civilian applications but was not adopted by the U.S. Army.

Tucker Sno-Cat T26E1 with steering skis and enclosure. (U.S. Army)

The Jeep

The ¼-ton, 4 × 4 truck (Jeep) was widely used by the military in World War II, with over 1.5 million made. Jeeps were delivered to the 10th Mountain Division consistent with the number authorized by the Ordnance Department. The American Bantam Motor Company originally designed and manufactured the Jeep, called the Bantam Jeep. However, due to the government's assessment that Bantam did not have the production capacity to deliver the number of Jeeps required, production was shifted to Ford and Willys-Overland. Bantam was relegated to making Jeep trailers. Jeeps were used for various jobs with the 10th, such as hauling supplies, medical evacuation, reconnaissance, and transport for commanders. These vehicles were issued to the 10th Mountain Division without the ski adapters.

88th Infantry Division and 10th Recon Jeeps in Italy.

10th Medical Jeeps in Italy.

¼-Ton 4 × 4 Truck, Willys Model MB (TM 10-1513)	
Engine Type	Gasoline
Number of cylinders	4
Bore	3⅛ in.
Stroke	4⅜ in.
Piston displacement	134.2 cu. in.
Compression ratio	6.48:1
Horsepower S.A.E.	15.6
Horsepower actual	60
Revolutions per minute	4,000
Torque maximum	105 ft. lb.
Revolutions at maximum torque	2,000 rpm
Wheelbase	80 in.
Tread	48¼ in.; with combat wheels 49 in.
Length	132¾ in.
Overall height normal load	
To top of cowl	40 in.
To top of steering wheel	51¼ in.
Top up	69¾ in.
Weight maximum payload	800 lb.
Maximum trailed load	1,000 lb.
Shipping weight (less water, fuel, and chains)	2,125 lb.
Road weight	2,315 lb.
Gross weight	3,125 lb.

Dash on a 1944 Willys MB Jeep.

Military Police Jeep outside Camp Hale on U.S. Route 24. Note the engine compartment cover to retain heat. (John Adams-Graf)

1945 Willys MB Jeep.

Snow Tractor T29

Left front view of Snow Tractor T29 Willys Jeep adapted with add-ons such as a track set and rear box. (U.S. Army)

Right front view of Snow Tractor T29E1, a Willys Jeep adapted with additional equipment such as a track set, front skis, and rear box. (The ski adapters were not used by the 10th Mountain Division.) (U.S. Army)

Side view of Snow Tractor T29 Willys Jeep adapted with add-ons such as a track set, front skis, and rear box. (U.S. Army)

Jeep M100 Trailer

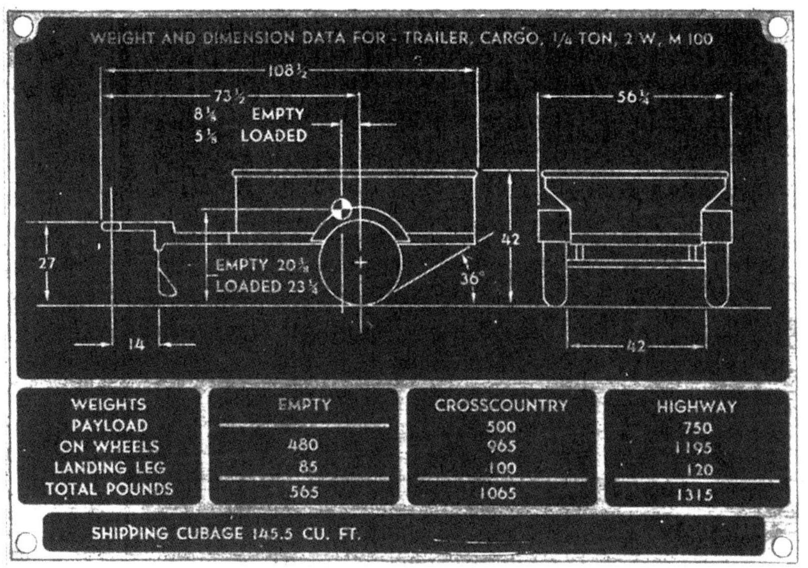

WEIGHTS	EMPTY	CROSSCOUNTRY	HIGHWAY
PAYLOAD		500	750
ON WHEELS	480	965	1195
LANDING LEG	85	100	120
TOTAL POUNDS	565	1065	1315

SHIPPING CUBAGE 145.5 CU. FT.

M100 Jeep trailer data plate. (TM 9-871A)

M100 Jeep trailer, right rear view.

The M100 Jeep trailer was a ¼-ton trailer towed by a ¼-ton Jeep. Several manufacturers built the M100 Jeep trailer. The American Bantam Motor Company manufactured 75,000 trailers and continued to do so after the war. Willys-Overland built 6,000 trailers. The trailer weighed approximately 565 lb., was 72 in. by 38 in., and was provided with Jeeps.

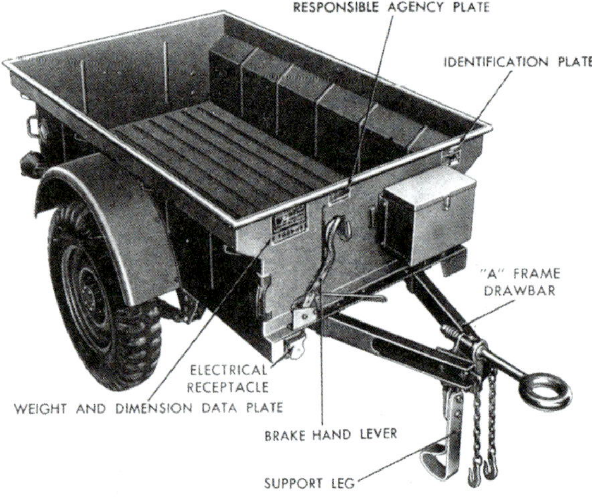

Right front view of M100 trailer. (TM 9-871A)

Left rear view of M100 trailer. (TM 9-871A)

Crosley Pup

Crosley was a small, independently owned automobile company specializing in small, lightweight vehicles. The company offered the Pup to the military as a competitor to the Jeep, but it was never adopted as a standard. It was too small. Anyone over 6 ft. could not fit in it.

Crosley Pup with driver Bjarne Martin testing the vehicle at Camp Hale. The fenders were made of canvas. The vehicle was very cramped for anyone over 6 ft. tall. (John Adams-Graf)

The Crosley mule prototype was not adopted by the 10th Mountain Division. (John Adams-Graf)

Left front view of a Crosley Pup. (John Adams-Graf)

Crosley Pups at the high country of Camp Hale, 1943. (U.S. Army)

Vehicles Used by the 10th Mountain Division from Other Units

The Weasel and the Jeep were the primary vehicles assigned to and used by the 10th Mountain Division. This chapter deals with selected vehicles and landing craft assigned from other units: the DUKW, the LCVP Higgins Boat, the 2½-ton truck, and the WC-51/52 Weapons Carrier.

The DUKW

At the beginning of World War II, the Ordnance Department identified a need for an amphibious vehicle to ferry troops and supplies across bodies of water or from transport ships to shore. General Motors Corporation was approached to supply the running gear, and Sparkman & Stephens yacht designers designed the tub. The running gear was that of a 2½-ton truck. DUKWs were relatively seaworthy if all hatches were closed and the large bilge pump was operational. DUKWs crossed the English Channel during the war. Approximately 21,000 DUKWs were manufactured during World War II.

DUKWs crossing the Po River in Northern Italy. The DUKW on the right has a crane mounted on the stern to lift heavy cargo, such as artillery and ammunition, from other DUKWs. (U.S. Army)

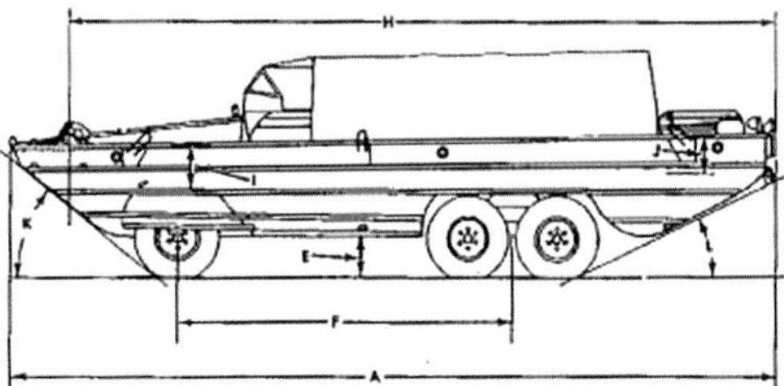

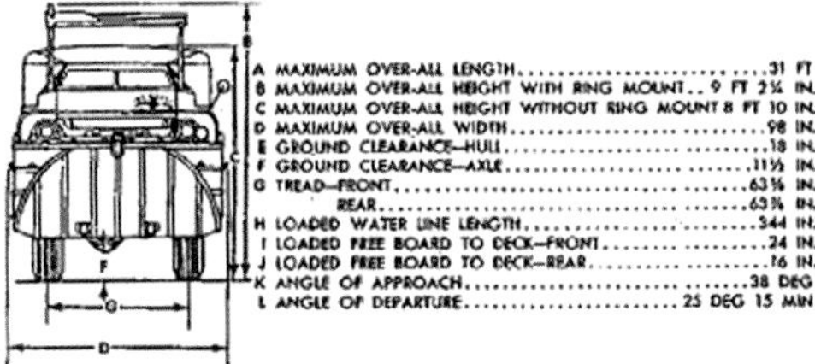

Vehicle Dimensional Views

c. Weights (approx.) (without ring mount).

	Prior to Chassis Serial No. 2006	Chassis Serial No. 2005 to 2506	After Chassis Serial No. 2505
Chassis, hull, fuel, oil, and water (lb)	13,610	13,950	14,320
Equipment (lb)	560	560	560
Total weight fully equipped (lb)	14,170	14,510	14,880
Driver (lb)	175	175	175
Payload (lb)	5,000	5,000	5,000
Gross weight (lb)	19,315	19,655	20,055

d. Engine Data.

Type	Valve-in-head
Number of cylinders	6
Bore	$3\frac{25}{32}$ in.
Stroke	4 in.
Piston displacement (cu in.)	269.5
Weight (without accessories)	572 lb

Technical data on the DUKW: The vehicle was geared very low to crawl out of a steep beach or overcome the operating load experienced while driving on loose sand. Tire pressure could be adjusted via an onboard compressor connected to swivel connectors on the wheels. (TM 9-802, 23 February 1945)

Driver's Compartment

A Windshield Regulators
B Left Hand Windshield Wiper
C Caution and Instruction Plates
D Flash Light
E Winch Cable Guide
F Map Compartment
G Right Hand Windshield Wiper
H First Aid Kit
I Front Clamp for Gun Mount
J Instrument Panel
K Horn Button
L Clutch Pedal
M Brake Pedal
N Accelerator Pedal
O Starter Button
P Air Scoop Regulator
Q Bilge Pump Valve Control Levers
R Winch Control Lever
S Tire Pump Control Lever
T Marine Propeller Control Lever
U Hand Brake Lever
V Gear Shift Lever
W Transfer Case Control Lever
X Front Axle Shift Lever

View of the driver's compartment. The hot radiator air exhaust was next to the windshield, and it tended to mix with the cooling air entering the floor grates in the driver's compartment, resulting in a hot ride in the summer. (TM 9-802, 15 October 1942)

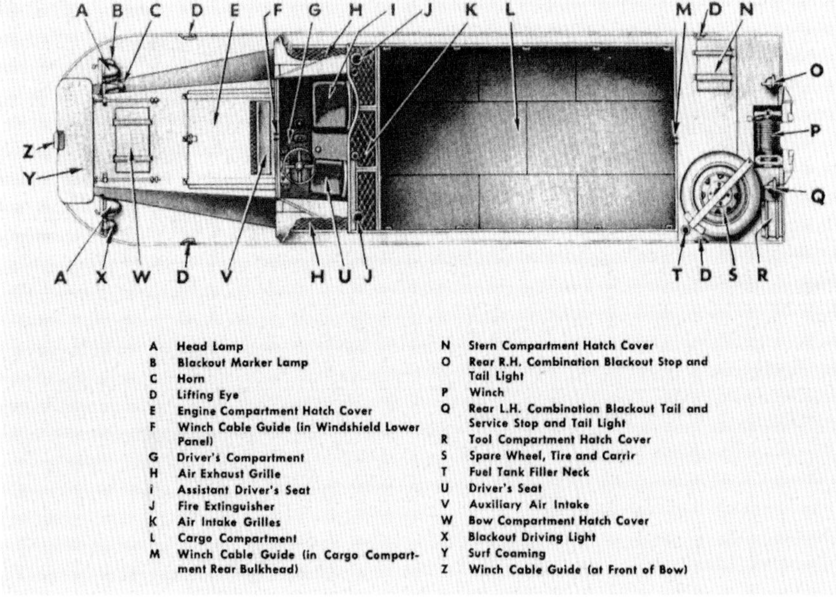

Top view of early model DUKW. (TM 9-802, 15 October 1942)

Truck, Amphibian, 2½-ton, 6 × 6 (TM 9-2800)			
General Data			
Crew			2
Weight			
Net			14,500 lb.
Payload			5,000 lb.
Gross			19,850 lb.
Shipping dimensions			248 sq. ft.
Tires	Ply 10		11.00 × 18
Tread, center to center (in.)	Front 63.56		Rear 63.88
Ground clearance			11¼ in.
Life preservers	Jacket type		5
Life ring			1
Loaded waterline length			344 in.
Loaded freeboard			
At coaming	Front 29 in.		Rear 29 in.
At deck	Front 24 in.		Rear 16 in.
Loaded draft	At front wheels 42 in.		At rear wheels 51 in.
Cargo space (cu. ft.)			
To top of coaming 198			Under tarp with bows 385
Electrical system			6 volts
Capacities:	Fuel, 70 octane gasoline		40 gal.
	Cooling system		20 qt.
	Crankcase (refill)		10 qt.
Pintle height			48 in.
Brakes			Hydraulic (Hydrovac)
Performance			
Maximum gradability			60%
Turning radius: Land (ft.)		Left 36	Right 35
Water		Left 17½	Right 12½
Angle of approach			38°
Angle of departure			25°

Cruising range:	Land					240 mi.
	Water top speed, 2nd gear					30 mi.
	Water cruising speed, 3rd gear					50 mi.
Maximum allowable speed (mph):		1st	2nd	3rd	4th	5th
	Land	7	11	12	40	50
	Water		6.4	5.4		
Engine						
Manufacturer					GMC	Model 270
Type						In-line, 4 cycle, 6 cylinders
Displacement						269½ cu. in.
Brake horsepower						104
Ignition type						Battery
Winch capacity						10,000 lb.

DUKW Sinking at Lake Garda

Activated in 1942, the 10th Mountain Division was stationed at Camp Hale in Colorado. The 87th Regiment took part in the operation to retake the island of Kiska in the Aleutian Islands, Alaska, in August 1943. In January 1945, the division was transported to Italy, assigned to the Fifth Army, and deployed opposite the border of the Tuscany and Emilia-Romagna regions.

The 10th Mountain Division attacked and broke through the German defensive lines on Monte Belvedere. The offensive lasted from February to March 1945, during which the division controlled the main road to Porretta. During the following mid-April offensive, the 10th Mountain Division reached the Po Valley (Pianura Padana) and arrived at the Po River on April 22, 1945. The division advanced to Verona on April 26 with the objective of stopping the German retreat.

It was common toward the war's end to restructure units into task forces to handle specific missions. General George Hays, the division commander, initiated Task Force Darby under the direction of Colonel William Darby. Darby was to take the 86th Mountain Infantry Regiment as the lead unit, together with other units up the eastern shore of Lake Garda.

Led by the 86th Mountain Infantry, the task force traveled up the eastern Gardesana Road on April 27. It reached Malcesine and Navene next to the partially completed German defensive line in the Alps from Stelvio to Istria. The rapid Allied advance prevented the Germans from digging in and presenting a formidable defense. Leaving Navene on April 28, 1945, the 10th reached the tunnels on the Gardesana Road from Navene to Torbole. During their retreat through Northern Italy, the Germans usually destroyed bridges and tunnels. They had blown the tunnels to stall the advance. An amphibious assault along the shores of Lake Garda was the only means to bypass the tunnel blockages. However, the Fifth Army had anticipated this and had amassed several amphibious vehicles (DUKWs) to transport troops along the lake to bypass the German obstacles.

On the evening of April 28, the task force arrived at Tempesta and then liberated Torbole. On April 30, Task Force Darby rested while patrols were sent out to determine the retreating Germans' new location. Unfortunately, Darby was killed that day by an airburst from enemy artillery.

The 10th's new mission was to head from Torbole to Riva del Garda across Lake Garda using their amphibious DUKWs. The plan was to sail into the middle of the lake, rather than hug the shore, to avoid German artillery and sniper fire between Riva and Torbole, with the 85th and 86th Regiments taking the lead along the eastern shore of Lake Garda.

Three DUKWs were assigned to Batteries B and C of the 605th Field Artillery Battalion, which was attached to the 10th Mountain Division. Each DUKW was to carry a 75 mm pack howitzer, equipment, ammunition, and members of the artillery battalion. The pack howitzers were most likely disassembled into pieces that one or two soldiers could carry.

As all this equipment and personnel were loaded into the three DUKWs, DUKW driver PFC Nicholas Del Grosso of the 52nd Quartermaster Battalion that provided the vehicles voiced concern about overloading. Fully loaded, there was less than one foot of freeboard—the height from the water line to the top of the coaming board—on the DUKW he was piloting.

Del Grosso had good reason for concern. His DUKW had men from Batteries B and C, a pack howitzer weighing 1,500 lb., 75 mm ammunition, 27 men with 50 lb. backpacks, and a .50 cal. machine gun. Assuming each man weighed about 150 lb., the calculated weight would have been 6,900 lb, not including ammunition and the .50 cal. machine gun. The maximum load capacity for a DUKW was 5,000 lb. According to the operator's manual, 7,500 lb. could be loaded onto a DUKW *in an emergency* (italics added). PFC Kenneth Klahn of Battery C, 605th Field Artillery, was removed and sent to another DUKW, thereby reducing the load by approximately 200 lb.

The three DUKWs set out into Lake Garda, heading toward Riva del Garda on the evening of April 30. After a storm developed, PFC Del Grosso's DUKW encountered rough water about halfway through the voyage.

Because of the DUKW's low freeboard, the designers had anticipated that water could enter the vehicle in heavy seas. Consequently, a large bilge pump was provided that was chain-driven from the propeller shaft. It could quickly remove water from the bilge. According to the lone survivor, Corporal Thomas Hough, the engine quit during the sudden storm. Del Grosso thought water had gotten into the gasoline or flooded the engine compartment, which may have shorted out the ignition system or been ingested into the carburetor. Because the engine was not running, the bilge pump was not working.

According to Corporal Hough, Del Grosso opened the forward storage compartment at the bow of the craft to get his tools to check out the engine. The forward storage compartment did not allow access to the engine but, if flooded, had avenues for water to flow into the engine compartment. Normally, tools were not stored there because of the risk of puncturing the vehicle's radiator. Instead, they were stored in the driver's compartment.

While Del Grosso accessed the storage area, waves probably crashed over the sides, further flooding the hull. It became apparent that the DUKW was going to sink. Soldiers started throwing everything overboard, hoping to stay afloat, including their backpacks, the pack howitzer, the .50 cal. machine gun, and all the ammunition.

Their efforts were in vain. The vehicle rapidly sank, leaving the soldiers in the freezing-cold water. Several soldiers could not swim and drowned. Others who could float succumbed to the icy water and perished. A former lifeguard and strong swimmer, Hough was the sole survivor of the accident.

Four days later, on May 2, 1945, hostilities in Italy ended. The 25 soldiers who died in the sinking of the DUKW were among the last to die in Italy.

Analysis of the Sinking of the DUKW

The DUKW had a pusher radiator fan that drew air through the floor grating in the driver's compartment, then through the radiator, and then pushed the air forward through air tunnels and out vents on the side of the hull. The airflow area over the radiator was essentially that of the fan's diameter, unlike road vehicles that benefited from additional airflow from forward movement.

However, there was a design flaw in the early DUKWs. The air intake was located where water could easily enter the engine compartment and stall the engine. The auxiliary air intake door was designed to help get more air into the engine compartment and enhance airflow through the inlet openings in the engine compartment. The problem with the auxiliary air intake scoop was that it easily ingested water in heavy seas, causing the engine to quit and, in some cases, the DUKW to sink.

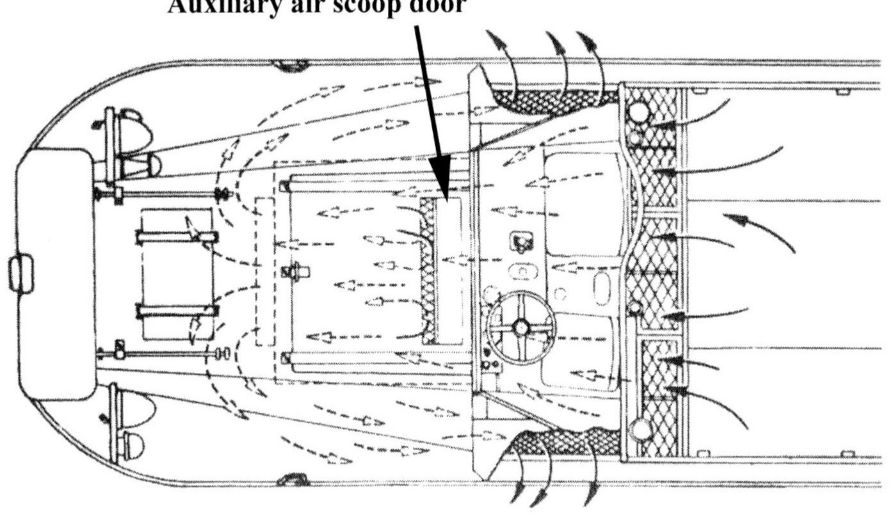

The cooling system on a DUKW was a pusher system where air was pushed forward through the radiator rather than drawn through the radiator, as in conventional land vehicles. The auxiliary air scoop allowed cooling air to go directly into the engine compartment, which helped cool but was a hazard when left open in heavy seas. (TM 9-802, September 1, 1943)

The auxiliary air scoop doors were opened and closed by moving a lever inside the driver's compartment. Without the engine running, the large bilge pump became inactive, making the vessel vulnerable to sinking. Furthermore, the DUKW's front deck was sloped downward. It was easily awash during heavy seas, allowing water to enter an open auxiliary air intake door. As early as 1943, several updates to U.S. Army TM 9-802 discussed the problems with the air scoop door allowing flooding of the engine compartment and what to do about it for vehicles equipped with these doors.

Often referred to as a "Duck," the DUKW was manufactured by General Motors. "DUKW" was a General Motors designation, with "D" indicating it entered service in 1942, "U" meaning it was a utility amphibious vehicle, "K" designating it as front-wheel drive, and "W" identifying it as having dual rear-driven axles.

The yacht designer, Sparkman & Stevens, engineered the tub to fit on the 2½-ton truck running gear of the standard GMC G-508 series of vehicles.

Often referred to as a "Duck," the GMC-manufactured DUKW combined the versatility of the 2½-ton 6 × 6 cargo truck while also being amphibious. This view of an unloaded, late-model DUKW shows the coaming board, an upward extension of the hull meant to reduce the chance of water entry.

In 2011, a group of Italian volunteer divers, *Gruppo Volontari del Garda*, located the ill-fated DUKW that sank in 1945. In 2018, ProMare, a team of experienced archaeologists and marine professionals, returned to Lake Garda to assist the local authorities in their efforts to monitor and preserve this important military gravesite. After a few successful dives using a manned submersible, the scientific team thoroughly investigated the site. The bow view of the ill-fated DUKW at the bottom of Lake Garda showed the auxiliary air scoop door open. This would have allowed water to enter the engine compartment directly, probably shorting out the ignition system and causing the engine to stop. The air scoop door should have been closed. (ProMare)

PFC Nicholas Del Grosso, the DUKW's driver, was worried that the engine compartment had flooded due to Lake Garda's rough waters. He was probably correct. A starboard-side view of the ill-fated DUKW shows the auxiliary air scoop door open. (ProMare)

View of the ill-fated DUKW at the bottom of Lake Garda showing the cargo compartment, which was empty. The plywood floorboards have floated away, showing the support framing and the bottom of the hull. According to Corporal Thomas Hough, the lone survivor, the soldiers were throwing everything overboard, as evidenced by photo—there is nothing in the cargo compartment. Due to the running gear and suspension system, the DUKW was very bottom-heavy, suggesting that it submerged like a submarine and did not roll over, settling to the bottom of the lake upright. (ProMare)

Bow view of the ill-fated DUKW showing the bow storage hatch open. According to Thomas Hough, PFC Del Grosso opened this hatch to get his tools to work on the engine. The open bow storage hatch allowed more water to enter the engine compartment, aggravating flooding and filling the bow with water, much like the *Titanic*. (ProMare)

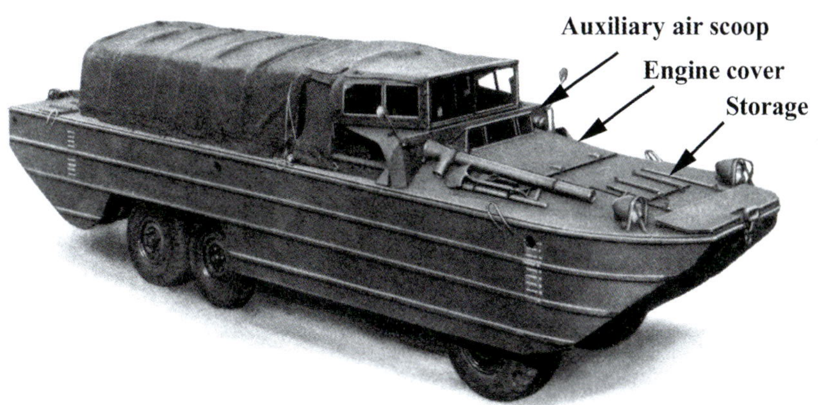

Right front view of an early model DUKW showing the auxiliary air scoop air intake, engine cover, and storage hatch. According to early technical manuals, closing the door on the air scoop was required during water operation. The air scoop air intake was eliminated from vehicles built after 1943 because, when left open, wave action would swamp the bow, water would enter the engine compartment and stall the engine. (TM 9-2800)

35. AIR CIRCULATION.

a. Cooling and Heating Air Circulation System Intake. Cooling air enters the engine compartment through air intake grilles located in aisle to rear of driver's compartment. The air is drawn forward under the driver's compartment into engine compartment by action of engine fan.

(1) NOTE: *Many of the vehicles are equipped with an auxiliary air scoop located directly in front of windshield on front deck. It has been found through experience that this auxiliary air intake is not necessary providing other air circulation controls are properly positioned. These scoops should be permanently fastened down and sealed as described in paragraph 228f.*

f. Auxiliary Air Intake Door (fig. 201). Additional cooling advantage by use of auxiliary air intake is offset by danger of stalling engine by shipping water through door. Therefore, it is recommended that door be permanently closed on vehicles prior to chassis serial No. 7136 (except Nos. 5671 through 6601) as follows:

(1) Raise engine compartment hatch cover. Remove entire auxiliary

TM 9-802
228-229

Maintenance Instructions

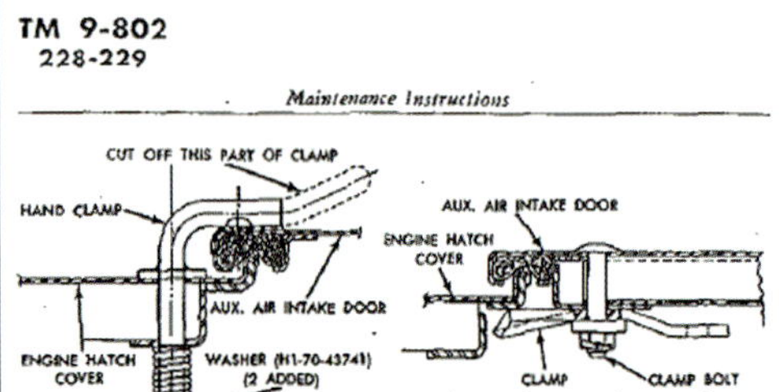

Figure 201—Auxiliary Air Intake Door Permanently Closed

air intake door operating mechanism including screen. Do not remove latches.

(2) Cover hole in upper toeboard with any suitable metal plate, attaching plate with screws. Remove "Auxiliary Cooling Air Intake" instruction plate from vehicle.

(3) Inspect air scoop door seal (G501-03-82791) and make any necessary repairs or replacements to insure a watertight seal.

(4) At under side of engine hatch cover, remove nuts, cotter pins from latch bolts. With latch in locked position, install ⅜-inch lock washer, install nut and cotter pin, and tighten securely to permanently close door. On vehicles with hand clamps (prior to chassis serial No. 2006), remove nuts. Install two additional ⅜-inch flat washers (HI-70-4371) on each bolt, then install nut. Make sure clamps are in proper position to lock hatch cover, then firmly tighten nuts to fully compress springs and secure with cotter pins. On vehicles prior to chassis serial No. 2006, cut off ends of clamps. Tack-weld clamps to door, using shielded arc. Avoid heating door sufficiently to burn seal.

Page from TM 9-802, February 23, 1945, showing how to permanently seal the air scoop on vehicles equipped with these doors.

The vehicle weighed approximately 14,500 lb. and was powered by a straight 6-cylinder, overhead valve engine generating approximately 100 horsepower. It could carry 25 soldiers or a load of up to 5,000 lb. at up to 50 mph on land and approximately 5 mph on water. Tire pressure could be changed from the driver's compartment to accommodate various beach conditions, such as sand or coral.

The Army instituted a design change in 1943 that eliminated the auxiliary air intake door on later models. In addition, it advised permanently sealing the air intake doors on older models. According to TM 9-802, issued on February 23, 1945, the Quartermaster Corps was supposed to seal all auxiliary air intake hatches shut. It is unknown why this was not accomplished on the ill-fated DUKW.

Additionally, despite being rated with a 5,000 lb. capacity, the ill-fated DUKW was carrying approximately 7,000 lb. While a load of up to 7,500 lb. could be tolerated in emergency conditions and calm water, Del Grosso was not facing "emergency conditions" before he drove the DUKW into Lake Garda. He was correct in objecting to the overloading.

Twenty-five soldiers drowned, some because they did not know how to swim, while others probably succumbed to the icy waters. Standard equipment for a DUKW included five life preservers. Lake Garda has a history of violent storms because of the difference in elevation of the lake with respect to the high mountains where cold air mixes with warmer air below. One could get away with overloading a DUKW with an open-air scoop in calm water but operating a DUKW in heavy seas was inviting disaster. It is not unusual for several factors to come together; these factors contributed to the loss of life from the sinking of the ill-fated DUKW—but it was an avoidable tragedy.

As seen in this photo of a late 1945-vintage DUKW, the auxiliary air intake (air scoop) doors have been removed from the design.

Lieutenant Colonel Woran, chaplain of the 10th Mountain Division, stands in the bed of a DUKW to lead a group of men in prayer at Torbole on May 3, 1945, the day following the unconditional surrender of all German troops in Italy. Not present were the 25 soldiers who died when their DUKW sank just days earlier. (National Archives)

Higgins Boat (LCVP)

During Operation *Cottage*, the campaign at Kiska, Alaska, the 87th Regiment from the Mountain Training Center, Camp Hale, Colorado, used LCVP (Landing Craft Vehicle Personnel) Higgins boats to go ashore. The LCVP was the ubiquitous troop landing craft of its day. Its capacity was approximately 36 soldiers or about 5,000 lb. of equipment.

The commercial ship *President Jackson* was launched in 1921 by Newport News Shipping and Dry-Dock Co. The U.S. Navy acquired the ship in 1940 and, in 1942, commissioned the ship as the USS *Zeilin*. The ship participated in campaigns in Alaska and the South Pacific; it was scrapped in May 1948. In April 1943, the *Zeilin* sailed for Cold Bay, Alaska, the rendezvous point for the Attu Island invasion force. On May 11, 1943, the *Zeilin* was anchored in Massacre Bay on the southern coast of Attu Island. After the initial landings, the *Zeilin* remained off Attu until mid-May, when she stopped at Adak, Alaska, on the way to San Diego, California, arriving on May 31. *Zeilin* returned to Adak in August 1943 for the Kiska invasion with the 87th Mountain Infantry Regiment. The ship later departed the Aleutians and arrived back at San Diego at the beginning of September.

Troopships, a destroyer, a Higgins Eureka Boat, and an LCVP at a harbor near Kiska.

Typical Landing Craft Vehicle Personnel (LCVP), Higgins Boat.

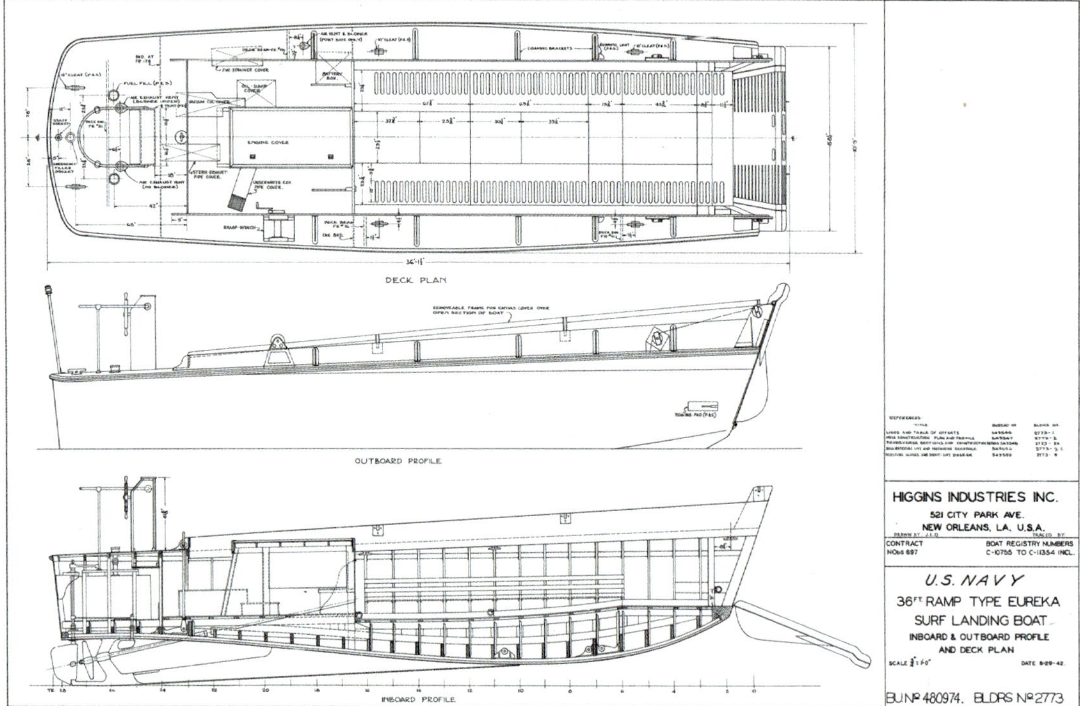

Detailed drawing of the Higgins LCVP.

The 87th Mountain Infantry Regiment was assigned to Amphibious Task Force 9 directly from the Mountain Training Center at Camp Hale, CO. A part of the 87th Regiment was aboard the *Zeilin* and transferred to LCVPs for the attack on Kiska. The captain of the ship was Commander Thomas B. Fitzpatrick. As the photograph on the following page shows, Higgins boats are lined up behind the jetty. During the attack on Kiska, these landing craft were lowered alongside the ship, and the 87th Mountain troops would crawl down a large net into them.

USS *Zeilin* (APA-3). (Wikimedia Commons)

Kiska patch representing the operation to retake the Aleutian Islands.

Trailer, cargo, 6-ton, tracked, Athey, model BT898-1. After-action reports state that the mud at Kiska was so severe that the only vehicles that moved were the D5 Caterpillars towing Athey trailers. Apparently, the M28s were also able to negotiate the mud with the Athey trailers in tow. (TM 9-370A)

Landing supplies on Kiska. This beach appears rocky, with several large rocks that blocked the way for an LCVP to land close to the beach. Consequently, the coxswain had to unload the LCVP in deeper water, and many of the 87th Regiment troops got wet while landing. In this environment with very cold conditions, getting wet could have serious medical consequences such as hypothermia. A bulldozer has constructed a jetty so that landing craft can dump their troops or cargo on the beach without getting wet. In some cases, if the water was too shallow for the LCVP to get close enough to shore to offload troops, a rubber boat would be brought alongside to ferry them ashore. The Weasel at the far right, with only its tracks and float gear showing, is towing an Athey 6-ton Tracked Trailer, probably secured from another unit. (John Adams-Graf)

Landing Craft Tanks (LCTs) on Kiska beach on August 8, 1943, unloading vehicles, supplies, and troops. Patrols are seen in the hills in the background. (U.S. Army)

If there were heavy seas, one had to time it when entering the boat. When the LCVP was rising because of a wave, it was not a good idea to jump in because the soldier would impact the deck of the LCVP more severely than waiting until the boat was at the top of the wave before jumping in. The soldier should not have his helmet chinstrap connected because if he fell into the water, he would choke or his neck would snap. Upon landing, the bow ramp of the LCVP dropped, and the troops ran out to either the left or right of the centerline to avoid getting run over by the landing craft because it got lighter when troops disembarked, and waves often carried it farther toward shore.

Troops at Kiska. On the far right is a member of the 87th Mountain Infantry Regiment. The soldier (far left) may be a member of one of the other units, such as the 1st Special Service Force. (John Adams-Graf)

2½-ton Truck

2½-ton truck. (Wikimedia Commons)

Truck, Cargo, 2½-ton, 6 × 4 (TM 9-2800)		
Crew		2
Weight without winch		9,635 lb.
Payload without winch		10,000 lb.
Gross without winch		19,635 lb.
Shipping dimensions	88 cu. ft. without winch	154 sq. ft.
	93 cu. ft. with winch	162 sq. ft.
Tires	8 ply	7.50 × 20
Tread, center to center	Front 66⅞ in.	Rear 67¾ in.
Ground clearance		10 in.
Pintle height	Loaded 30⅞ in.	Unloaded 32⅝ in.
Electrical system		6 volts
Capacities:	Fuel 70 octane gasoline	40 gal.
	Cooling system	21 qt.
	Crankcase	6½ qt.
Brakes		Hydraulic with booster
Performance		
Maximum gradability		30%
Turning radius	Right 34½ ft.	Left 35 ft.
Angle of approach	With winch 30°	Without winch 40°

	Angle of departure	44°
	Fuel consumption, average	5.9 mpg
	Maximum allowable speed	45 mph
	Number of speeds forward	5
	Winch capacity	10,000 lb.
Engine		
	Manufacturer	Hercules Model JXD
	Type	In-line, 4 cycle, 6 cylinder
	Displacement	320 cu. in.
	Governed engine speed	2,620 rpm
	Ignition type	Battery

In 1939, it became apparent that the U.S. Army should have a 2½-ton 6 × 6 truck available for hauling troops or transporting supplies. GMC submitted a bid for the ACKWX-353 truck based on GMC's commercial AC series trucks using the 256 cu. in. gasoline-fueled engine with 4-speed transmission. Approximately 2,466 ACKWX-353 trucks were built for the U.S. Army, and 1,000 trucks were built for the French government, which were delivered to England instead because of the fall of France.

ACKWX-353 2½-ton truck manufactured by GMC. This is an early model 2½-ton truck that was essentially a civilian truck, painted olive drab, with a radiator guard.

In 1940, the ACKWX-353 was upgraded to the CCKWX-353, which was designed with the military in mind. The "C" represents the model year 1941, with a larger 269½ cu. in. engine with a 5-speed transmission. Approximately 13,188 CCKWX-353 trucks were manufactured with a long or short wheelbase until early 1941. The next model CCKW, with all GMC parts, was called the first series. 41,188 vehicles were manufactured from 1941–45. The next model, called the second series, was a vehicle with a redesigned closed cab: models 1608 and 1609, which replaced models 1574 and 1575. Approximately 46,425 vehicles were manufactured between June 1941 and May 1942. The third series of CCKW manufacture comprised 126,038 vehicles produced from May 1942 to April 1943. Many changes were made during this production run, such as redesigned steering wheels and brush guards. The cab was changed from a closed cab to an open cab. The cargo box was changed from steel to wood. The fourth series had the open cab and wooden cargo body with 107,426 vehicles manufactured between April 1943 and January 1944. Examples of changes made include an improved cab top, larger windows on the door curtains, and large neck fuel fillers. The fifth series, produced between February 1944 and November 1944, entailed 73,499 vehicles. The thickness of frame members was increased, and additional reinforcements were made to the cargo body. The sixth series of 168,174 vehicles was manufactured between November 1944 and August 1945 with minor changes.

Truck, cargo, 2½-ton, 6 × 4. (TM 9-2800)

Vehicle illustrated above: Studebaker

Classification: Substitute standard

Purpose: To transport general cargo.

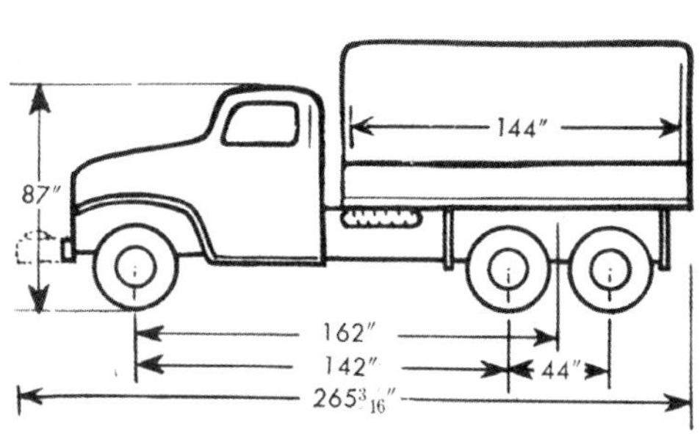

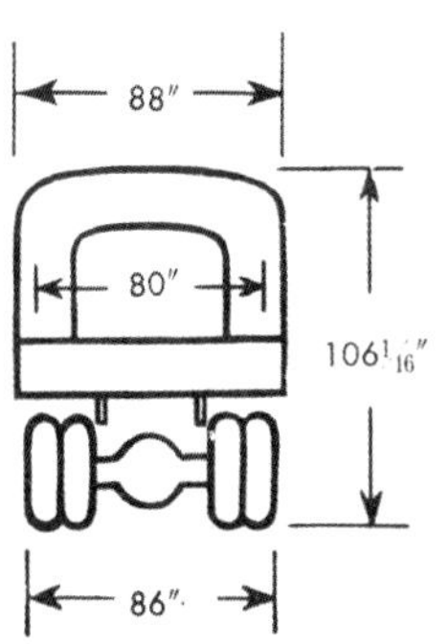

10th Mountain Division in Italy with a 2½-ton truck hauling troops.

Some 562,750 CCKW trucks were manufactured; production was stopped in August 1945. The main body types were cargo, dump, gasoline tanker, and water tanker. All the CCKW series were manufactured by the Yellow Truck & Coach Co. and later by the GMC Corporation at the Pontiac Michigan plant and the Chevrolet St. Louis plant. The Studebaker Corporation and IHC manufactured some 2½-ton trucks, but the CCKW production dominated this type of vehicle. GMC CCKW trucks with several body styles were given to allies through Lend-Lease.

The CCKW is a conventional all-wheel-drive truck designed for overland and unimproved roads. The clutch is a single-drive plate type connected to a 5-speed transmission and one reverse gear. The fourth gear is direct drive, and the fifth gear is overdrive. A 2-speed transfer case allows 4 × 6 operation and 6 × 6 operation. Power is transferred to three drive axles through a transfer case. A front-mounted winch with a 10,000 lb. capacity is connected to a power takeoff connection to the transmission. Service brakes are hydraulic with a vacuum-assisted hydrovac booster. The vehicle is equipped with an electric brake controller for towing artillery. The cab is a hard top with a two-man capacity for early vehicles and an open cab with a convertible top for later-model vehicles. The vehicle had nicknames: "Jimmy," "Deuce-and-a-Half," or the "Deuce."

WC-51 Weapons Carrier

WC-51 Weapons Carrier.

WC-52 Weapons Carrier, essentially a WC-51 with winch.

The Dodge Motor Corporation had been building trucks for the U.S. Army in the 1930s—the ½-ton 4 × 2 and 4 × 4 trucks. In 1939, Dodge won the contract for ½-ton 4 × 4 trucks for the U.S. Army. The contract was called the VC series, with six body types, VC-1 through VC-6 or the T-202 series. The "V" stood for the 1940 model year, which was changed to "W" for the 1941 design. The U.S. Army was dissatisfied with the performance of the T-202 series vehicles because of their high center of gravity and narrow body, resulting in difficulty in offroad terrain. On August 6, 1941, a prototype WC weapons carrier was received at Aberdeen Proving Grounds. This resulted in the development and production of several models, as shown below:

- WC-51 Weapons Carrier
- WC-52 Weapons Carrier with winch
- WC-53 Carryall
- WC-54 Ambulance
- WC-55 37 mm Gun Motor Carriage M6
- WC-56 Command Reconnaissance Car
- WC-57 WC-56 with winch
- WC-58 Radio Truck
- WC-59 Telephone Maintenance Truck
- WC-60 Emergency Repair Truck
- WC-61 Telephone Maintenance Truck
- WC-64 Ambulance

These WC models were based on the 4 × 4 chassis and were typical four-wheel-drive trucks, with a wide width and a relatively short wheelbase. These vehicles worked well on unimproved roads and cross-country with a full load towing a trailer or artillery piece. The Dodge T-214 6-cylinder gasoline engine developed 92 hp, providing power through a single dry disk-type clutch. The 4-speed transmission provided four speeds forward and one in reverse. The transmission was not of a synchromesh design, so double clutching was required to shift gears smoothly. A power take-off shaft on the left side of the transmission drove the winch at the front of the vehicle. A transfer case allowed the front wheels to be disconnected from the power train for two-wheel drive. There was no high or low range. Consequently, a typical speed for this vehicle was about 30 mph in fourth gear. Brakes were standard drum hydraulic brakes with no booster assembly. The weapons carriers had an open driver's compartment with two bucket seats and a canvas top. The cargo box had a set of three bows to support a canvas top. The spare wheel was mounted on the left side of the driver's compartment, making it difficult to exit the vehicle. The driver had to crawl over the passenger's seat to exit the vehicle. A pintle hook was available for towing vehicles. Six-wheel 1½-ton vehicles were also developed using the basic design of the WC with the designation WC-62 personnel and cargo, and WC-63, a WC-62 with a winch. These vehicles had two rear axles.

10th Mountain Division in Italy; a weapons carrier is in the lead hauling equipment.

Classification: Standard

Purpose: To transport weapons, tools and equipment.

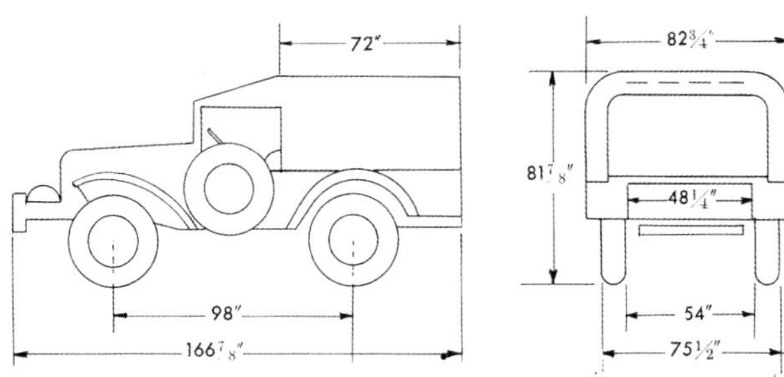

WC-52 dimensions. (TM 9-2800)

Truck Weapons Carrier, ¾-Ton, 4 × 4 (TM 9-2800)		
General Data		
Crew		2
Weight Net		5,250 lb.
Payload		1,500 lb.
Gross		6,750 lb.
Shipping dimensions	529 cu. ft.	102 sq. ft.
Tires:	Ply 8	9.00 × 16
Tread, center to center		64¾ in.
Ground clearance		10⅝ in.
Electrical system		6 volts
Capacities Fuel	70 octane gasoline	30 gal.
Cooling system		18 qt.
Crankcase (refill)		5 qt.
Brakes		Hydraulic
Performance		
Maximum gradability		60%
Turning radius		22 ft.
Fording depth		34 in.
Angle of approach	With winch 36°	Without winch 53°
Angle of departure		31°
Fuel consumption, average conditions		8 mpg
Cruising range, average conditions		240 mi
Maximum allowable speed		54 mph
Number of speeds forward		4
Engine		
Manufacturer		Dodge, Model T-214
Type	In-line 4 cycle	6 cylinders
Displacement		230.2 cu. in.
Governed speed		3,200 rpm
Brake horsepower		76
Ignition type		Battery
Winch capacity		5,000 lb.
For vehicles with winch, use the following data		
Weight Net 5,550 lb.	Payload 1,500 lb.	Gross 7,050 lb.

References

Adams-Graf, John, Photographic Collection of WWII 10th Mountain Division.

Conversations with Hugh Evans, 10th veteran WWII, at 10th Mountain Reunions, Leadville CO, 2005–19.

Conversations with Tiny McQuade, 10th veteran WWII, at 10th Mountain Reunions, Leadville CO, 2005–15.

Conversations with Robert Parker, 10th veteran WWII, at 10th Mountain Reunions, Leadville CO, 2005–07.

Conversations with John Woodward, 10th veteran WWII, at 10th Mountain Reunions, Leadville CO, 2005–14.

Eliason Snowmobiles, "The Early Years," http://www.eliason-snowmobile.com/, accessed February 6, 2024.

Eskelson, R. "A Comparison of Over-Snow Vehicles Produced at Utah State Agricultural College." Logan, Utah: Utah State University, master's thesis, 1955.

FM 23-5, U.S. Rifle, Caliber .30 M1, Department of the Army, May 1965.

FM 70-15, War Department, Basic Field Manual, Operations in Snow and Extreme Cold, November 1944.

Harris, Jeremiah, Photographic Collection of WWII 10th Mountain Division.

Imbrie, J. *Chronology of the 10th Mountain Division in World War II*. Watertown, New York National Association of the 10th Mountain Division, Inc., 2004.

Lang, Otto. *Downhill Skiing*. New York, New York: Holt & Company, 1936.

Little, Dave, Photographic Collection of WWII 10th Mountain Division.

OQMG Circular No. 4, Revised August 1943, U.S. Army Quartermaster Supply Catalog.

Parareda, C. "The Search for Fallen Heroes, Lake Garda, Italy." IEEE Xplore, 2019.

ProMare 2018 Expedition to Lake Garda, https://promare.org/projects/archive-italy/archive-italy-lake-garda/ accessed January 18, 2024.

Roberts, Charles C. Jr., WWII Collection including photographs.

The DUKW: Its Operation and Uses, U.S. Army Circular N-4477, 1944.

TM 9-246, War Department Technical Bulletin, 37-MM Gun T32 and Tripod Mount T9, 10 August 1944.

TM 9-303, War Department Technical Manual, 57-MM Guns M1 and MK. III (British) and Carriages M1, M1A1, M1A2, M1A3, and M2, 25 April 1944.

TM 9-314, Department of the Army Technical Manual, 57-mm Rifles T15E13 and M18, 75-mm Rifles T21 and M20 (T25), March 1949.

TM 9-319, Department of the Army Technical Manual, 75mm Pack Howitzer M1A1 and Carriage M8, November 1943.

TM 9-325, Army Technical Manual, 105 mm Howitzer M2A1, Department of the Army, May 1948.

TM 9-772, War Department Technical Manual, Cargo Carriers M29 and M29C, 4 August 1945.

TM 9-774, War Department Technical Manual, Snow Tractor M7 and 1-Ton Snow Trailer M19, 31 January 1944.

TM 9-790A, 6-Ton Trailers (Athey), War Dept., December 1942.

TM 9-802, Technical Manual, Truck, Amphibian, 2½-ton, 6x6, GMC DUKW-353, War Department, 15 October 1942.

TM 9-802, Technical Manual, 2½-ton Amphibian Truck, 6x6, GMC DUKW-353, War Department, 1 September 1943.

TM 9-802, Technical Manual, 2½-ton, 6x6, Amphibian Truck, (GMC DUKW-353), War Department, 23 February 1945.

TM 9-871A, Department of the Army Technical Manual, ¼-Ton 2-Wheel Cargo Trailer M100, July 1951.

TM 9-893, Technical Manual, Light Cargo Carrier T-15, War Department, February 5, 1943.

TM 9-1325, Army Technical Manual, 105 mm Howitzer M2A1, Carriages M2A1 and M2A2; and Combat Vehicle Mounts M3 and M4; War Department, 21 September 1944.

TM 9-1774, War Department Technical Manual, Snow Tractor M7 and 1-Ton Snow Trailer M19, 17 April 1944.

TM 9-2200, War Department Technical Manual, Instruction Guide Small Arms Data, June 12, 1942.

TM 9-2800, Technical Manual, Standard Military Motor Vehicles, War Department, 1 September 1943.

TM 10-1513, Maintenance Manual for Willys Truck, Willys-Overland Motors, Inc., Toledo, Ohio, May 1942.

U.S. Army Signal Corps WWII photos, National Archives.

U.S. Patent 2,323,526, C. J. E. Eliason, 6 July 1943.

Whitlock, F. *Soldiers on Skis: A Pictorial Memoir of the 10th Mountain Division*. Boulder, Colorado: Paladin Press, 1992.

Wzolek, Jeff, WWII Photographic Collection.

Index